THE REAL READER'S QUARTERLY

Slightly Foxed

'A Private, Circumspect People'

NO.11 AUTUMN 2006

Publisher and co-editor Gail Pirkis
Co-editor Hazel Wood
Marketing Kathleen Smith
Publicity Stephanie Allen

Cover illustration by John Holder, with apologies to Gainsborough

John Holder was born in 1941 in Baldwell Ash, Suffolk, and studied at the Cambridge School of Art where he is now visiting lecturer in illustration. His work has been published in books and periodicals worldwide and he has exhibited his travel drawings in London and Dubrovnik.

Design by Octavius Murray

Layout by 875 Design

Colophon by David Eccles

Published by Slightly Foxed Limited
67 Dickinson Court
15 Brewhouse Yard
London ECIV 4JX

tel 020 7549 2121/2111
fax 0870 1991245
e-mail all@foxedquarterly.com
www.foxedquarterly.com

Slightly Foxed is published quarterly in early March, June, September and December
Annual subscription rates (4 issues)
UK £32; Europe £37; Rest of the World £42
Single copies of this issue can be bought for £8 (UK) or £10 (overseas)
Back issues are also available

ISBN 0-9551987-3-9
ISBN 978-0-9551987-3-1

Printed and bound by Smith Settle, Yeadon, West Yorkshire

Contents

From the Editors

It's one of those pleasant moments when nothing very particular is happening in the office. Pugwash the cocker spaniel is snoring in the late summer sunshine by the terrace window, a splendid helper is stuffing envelopes on the kitchen table, and from time to time the phone rings with a request for a slipcase or a subscription. Or it may be one of you just ringing in for a chat, which is always delightful. It's a golden, meditative time, when the summer's nearly over and the madness of the Christmas season hasn't begun.

So perhaps it is, in fact, a good time to get ahead with Christmas. When it comes to bookish friends and relatives, you might consider taking out a gift subscription to *Slightly Foxed* – possibly even adding one of our distinguished grey slipcases. They're going like hot cakes, we're delighted to say, and sales have far exceeded our expectations. Back issues are a good present, too, for recent subscribers, and four back issues in a slipcase make a very handsome gift.

Flushed with the success of our first excursion into 'merchandizing', and encouraged by your comments on our covers, we're now offering four of them as postcards, plus (by popular request) David Eccles's splendid version of *A Curse Against Book Stealers* which appeared in Issue 9. Interesting postcards, in our experience, are incredibly useful and quite hard to find, and we can see that *A Curse Against Book Stealers* has a number of practical applications too! For further details see the advertisement on p.96.

There's also another little 'Christmas Fox' on the way. A great many of you bought and enjoyed last year's *Ghost Writer*. This year's *The Reluctant Biographer* by Jeremy Lewis is equally delightful but very different – a lighthearted look at the author's unexpected second career as the authorized biographer of Cyril Connolly (among others). Any of you who have read *Kindred Spirits*, his hilarious account of his first career in publishing, will know what a treat this year's Christmas Fox is going to be – the perfect small present or special Christmas card. We'll be sending you details shortly.

If you're in the vicinity and feel like picking any of these items up in person, please do call. We're always delighted to see subscribers, on any pretext, or no pretext at all. The landmark to look out for is a pub called The Slaughtered Lamb, on the corner of Great Sutton Street, EC1 (we hope David Eccles's drawing will help you to identify it). Turn into Northburgh Street when you reach the pub, and the entrance to Dickinson Court is about 50 yards along on your left.

GAIL PIRKIS

HAZEL WOOD

Local directions,
by David Eccles

A Private, Circumspect People

MAGGIE FERGUSSON

Shortly after the end of the Second World War, the Royal Society of Literature took out a long lease on a white stucco Bayswater house, formerly the home of General Sir Ian Hamilton, leader of the Gallipoli Expedition. It was dilapidated but spacious, and a first-floor room roughly the size and shape of a tennis court became a library in which the Society's Fellows could browse among one another's works. All went well until, in the early Seventies, an elderly, light-fingered Fellow took to leaving the building with volumes secreted between two pairs of trousers, which he wore sewn together at the hem. The library was closed.

I began working for the Royal Society of Literature in the autumn of 1991, and it was on the shelves of this silent, abandoned room that I first discovered *Akenfield: Portrait of an English Village*. Published in 1969, it had become an instant classic, and, since then, it has never been out of print. From the first sentence – 'The village lies folded away in one of the shadow valleys which dip into the East Anglian coastal plain' – it was clear that this was a book to slow down for, and to relish.

It is now nearly forty years since Ronald Blythe, equipped with a tape recorder and an old Raleigh bicycle, travelled around the Suffolk countryside he had known from boyhood, capturing the memories and reflections of three generations of a rural community, to which he gave the imaginary name 'Akenfield' (*acen* is old English for 'oak').

Ronald Blythe, *Akenfield* (1969)
Penguin · Pb · 288pp · £9.99 · ISBN 0141187921

Akenfield, by Mary Kuper

These he transcribed, weaving them together with observations in his own precise, poetic prose.

That particular moment in the mid-Sixties provided an extrordinary vantage point from which to look both deep into the past and well into the future. The older villagers – 'The Survivors', as Blythe calls them – are steeped in a lore and a way of life that reach back hundreds of years. They talk of the ancient bond between ploughman and horse, and of how they sang to their beasts as they worked the fields. They recall their grandparents hurrying to inform the bees when a villager died, and hanging the hives with black crêpe – 'if you didn't, the bees would die as well'. They regret the new prevalence of steel, and the passing of the old method of smelting iron with charcoal to make strong, bright nails such as would have been used at the Crucifixion.

Despite their huge skies and wide horizons, they are a private, circumspect people, and they deliver their memories with a guarded matter-of-factness which occasionally blossoms into poetry. 'He walked smartly down the lane until his red coat was no bigger than a poppy,' says one retired farm-worker, recalling his brother's departure for the Boer War. 'Then the tree hid him. We never saw him again.' 'We dreaded the rain,' remembers Fred Mitchell, a retired horseman. 'It washed our few shillings away.'

But the old speech and the old ways were dying fast by the summer of 1967. Farming had become 'the agricultural industry', and for those who chose to remain on the land – and many did not – Walls and Birds Eye were the new masters. The gentle, reassuring sounds of 'larks, clocks, bees, tractor hummings' are punctuated, as Blythe bicycles about, by automatic bird-scarers exploding across the pea fields like minute guns. The pressure to maximize the return from the land means that animals are no longer allowed to roam on their old pastures, but pass their short lives locked up in sheds. Dr Tim Swift, the vet, speaks chillingly of how boredom and bewilderment are driving battery pigs and hens to cannibalism. The pigs chew off one another's tails; the poultry go further. 'First they pick a feather and taste blood, and soon some poor hen is disembowelled. It is a frequent thing.'

Yet *Akenfield* is not exactly a lament for the past. 'The Survivors' describe a turn-of-the-century life of such unremitting toil that nostalgia seems a Marie Antoinette indulgence. Leonard Thompson, aged 71, tells how his father, a farm labourer, brought up ten children on 13s a week. They were always hungry, and almost always thirsty. The nearest drinking water was at the foot of a hill a mile's walk away. He describes trying to slake his thirst one hot afternoon by swigging down the soapy water in which his mother had just done the week's washing. Every minute that he was not at school, he and his siblings were required to help with stone-picking in the fields. As soon as he left school, at 13, he took a job with a local farmer singling mangolds: sixty hours' work each week, for 3s. 'I want to say this simply as a fact,' Thompson states, 'that village people in Suffolk in my day were worked to death.'

In 1914, with two other boys from the village, he fled the wretchedness of rural life for the army, and was sent to the Dardanelles. On the shore, as they landed, was a huge marquee. It reminded them of the annual village fête, so they rushed towards it. Inside were hundreds of dead Englishmen, laid out in rows, their eyes wide open. 'I thought of Suffolk,' Thompson comments, 'and it seemed a happy place for the first time.'

Happiness, *Akenfield* illustrates, is relative, and rare. By the mid-Sixties, Akenfield is the kind of place weary urban dwellers dream of, with all the emblems of the English village idyll: 'A tall old church on the hillside, a pub selling the local brew, a pretty stream, a football pitch, a handsome square vicarage with a cedar of Lebanon shading it, a school with jars of tadpoles in the window . . .' Yet for all their 'modern' comforts – fitted carpets, central heating, deep-freezes, cars – most of the younger inhabitants of the village betray an unease quite unknown to their forefathers in the days of semi-feudal toil.

Some yearn for the past. Christopher Falconer, a gardener, spent the first fourteen years of his working life in service to Lord and Lady Covehithe in the big house on the borders of the village. He describes a set-up of *Through the Looking Glass* oddness, in which the indoor staff were required to turn their faces to the wall when their employers passed, and 'her Ladyship' would appear out of nowhere when he was at work in the garden and shout 'Swing your arms!' 'We gave, they took,' he states. 'It was the complete arrangement.' Yet, now that it is gone, he mourns it: 'I am a young man who has got stuck in the old ways. I am thirty-nine and I am a Victorian gardener, and this is why the world is strange to me.'

Others are overcome with anxiety about the future, unable to shake off the twentieth-century compulsion to 'get on': 19-year-old Brian Newton has dreamed from boyhood of working on a farm, but now that he is doing so, he frets. What will he be doing when he is 30? Or even 40? The older men working with him tell him that they didn't think like this – 'But I must. At the moment I can't see any climb or development however hard I work. If I stay I am already where I shall always be.'

Even in those for whom the present appears to be prosperous and full of promise, there is angst. Gregory Gladwell, the blacksmith, has managed to survive the great transition from horse to tractor which spelt ruin for most forges. Newcomers to the village, prepared to spend extortionate sums 're-garnishing' their houses and recreating 'original' fireplaces, troop to him with orders for weather-vanes, copper canopies, firedogs, firebacks, brass and pewter ornaments, light-brackets. He is overwhelmed not just with work, but with a nagging guilt about the uses to which he is putting his craft. Is he breaking faith with 'the old ones', his ancestors who shod the old farmhorses and made ploughs 'in the seventeen-somethings – *and on this very floor*?' 'I wasn't born soon enough,' Gladwell reflects, 'that's the trouble. By rights, I should be dead and gone. I think like the old people.'

When, half way through the book, we are introduced to Horry Rose, the saddler, and told that he is a 'happy man', it comes as something of a shock. Can it be so? Is *anybody* really happy?

Amidst this cast, Blythe maintains a discreet but sharp-eyed presence, able to evoke in two or three brisk brushstrokes a place, a situation or a character. When, for example, he introduces Marian Carter-Edwardes, 50, Samaritan, JP, Vice-Chairman of the Women's Institute – 'Surrounded by large dogs and good furniture. Nothing too much trouble. Racy, nothing could surprise her. Good-looking and moves with a girlish, tennis-court freedom. Drives a fast car with dogs looking out of the windows' – we know immediately what we are dealing with.

Blythe can be wry, but he is also unfailingly sensitive, and he is at his very best dealing with the more vulnerable members of the community, those living friendless and on the fringes. Michael Poole works in the Akenfield orchards. At 37, he cannot read or write a single letter. 'Simple' is how local people describe him, emphasizing the word in such a way as to make it clear that he is in no way frightening. But 'simple', Blythe explains, 'is exactly what he is not . . . There is no rest in that "simple" face, it has the alertness of a forest creature, eyes seizing at every object.'

Lana Webb, 23, is incontinent, and lives, unvisited by the other villagers, with her Gran. Their cottage is spotless – the lino 'translucent, like sucked toffee, its pattern all licked off by the duster'. After Blythe has sat with them for some time, they agree to show him their secret. A door is opened to reveal a long, white room, with the windows open and the wind hurtling through. 'It is blowing some twenty pairs of knickers. Pink, white, blue, flowered, plain, nylon, cotton, they jig happily above a galvanised zinc bath in which sheets are steeping. Gran closes the door and Lana, her expression faintly amused and challenging now, rises from her chair and goes off somewhere to change.'

Most movingly of all, in the final pages, we are introduced to 'Tender' Russ, the gravedigger. A widower, living alone with two budgies, 'Boy' and 'Girl', he inveighs so wildly against God and man, and against the uncertainties of life, that the other villagers give him a wide berth. His garden is a metaphor for the futility of his rages – 'Rows of sprouts have rotted until they have become yellow pustulate sticks; potatoes have reached up as far as they could go and fallen back into faded tangles'. In his cottage, he has retreated into one cluttered room. Only among the dead does he feel at ease. He keeps the names of all those he has buried in an address book, and meticulous records of where and *how* they lie. But for himself he wants no such comforts: 'I want to be cremated and my ashes thrown in the air. Straight from the flames to the winds, and let that be that.'

Returning to *Akenfield* fifteen years on, it is the balance between observation and compassion, epitomized in the meeting with 'Tender' Russ but running throughout the book, that makes it so memorable, and so moving. Blythe's aim, as set out in the introduction, was to capture 'the voice of Akenfield, Suffolk, as it sounded during the summer and autumn of 1967'. But he has achieved something more than this. As the final pieces of his mosaic are put into place, the village becomes a microcosm of the whole world, and one is left with feelings of tenderness, perplexity, wonder, not just for the inhabitants of a small corner of East Anglia, caught at a particular moment, but for the human condition.

MAGGIE FERGUSSON is Secretary to the Royal Society of Literature. Her first book, *George Mackay Brown: The Life*, was published in April.

Sheds and Watersheds

MIKE PETTY

When Professor Lisa Jardine was conducting her search for the 'essential male novel' among 400 men from the worlds of academia, the arts, publishing and literary criticism she unaccountably didn't get round to me. Not that my answer would have changed anything. The only surprising thing about the winner, *The Outsider* (*L'Étranger*) by Albert Camus, was that anybody was at all surprised.

Professor Jardine worried over the fact that her 400 men seemed curiously reluctant to admit to having what she called 'a watershed moment' where fiction was concerned, displaying 'a certain angst about revealing that fiction has had any impact on their day-to-day lives'. I'm not surprised that they clammed up when asked which novel 'played a part in making them the men they are today'; on the whole men, even literary critics, are happier in sheds than watersheds. (I myself am deeply puzzled by the fact that enough men thought that *The Hobbit* played a part in making them the men they are today to put it at joint fourth.)

The flat, unadorned narrative voice of *The Outsider* (the Americans called it *The Stranger*, but that seems all wrong) belongs to Meursault, a clerkly sort who lives and works in Oran, Algeria, in the late 1930s. As the novel opens he has just heard of the death of his mother. He travels to her funeral, though his main concern seems to be with how his boss will react to his taking extra time off. On his return he goes swimming, picks up a girl called Marie on the beach

---

Albert Camus, *The Outsider* (1942) · Translated by Joseph Laredo

Penguin · Pb · 188pp · £7.99 · ISBN 0141182504

and goes to bed with her. A neighbourhood pimp, Raymond, asks his advice about an Arab girl who has been two-timing him and needs to be taught a lesson. Raymond eventually beats her up, which brings him (and therefore Meursault, who has allowed himself to be dragooned into friendship with Raymond) into conflict with the girl's brother.

There is a confrontation on the beach, and knives are produced. Raymond is injured, and Meursault, dazed by the heat and the confusion, ends up shooting one of the Arabs in cold blood. At his trial much is made of his unemotional behaviour at his mother's funeral, his lack of remorse at his crime, his refusal to take any of the proffered escape routes. We leave him contemplating his impending execution with what you might call a howl of contentment.

I see from the inscription in my worn grey Penguin that I bought *The Outsider* in early 1963, between the end of the Chatterley ban and the Beatles' first LP, conveniently enough. That was rather early for me, unlike Larkin, and I dimly perceived that the florid (not to say floral) dalliances of Connie and Mellors were not how it was actually going to be. Not least among the many things that struck me forcibly on first reading *The Outsider* was Meursault's offhand bedding of Marie; the notion that you could Go All the Way with a girl without months of wheedling, merely by letting your hands stray over her breasts, was a novel and exciting one, if dangerously misleading. The hedonism that held sway in Oran in the late '30s still hadn't reached Southend-on-Sea by the early '60s.

But *The Outsider* wasn't about sex, it was about telling the truth – or refusing to lie, a much more potent way of looking at it. The novel's famously placid (and carefully punctuated) first line – 'Mother died today. Or, maybe, yesterday; I can't be sure.' – seemed to me a perfectly reasonable response to an ambiguous telegram. That you could end up in the condemned cell, not just for killing an Arab in a moment of inadvertence, but for failing to greet the death of your mother with the correct display of filial emotion, was terrifying but not surprising. The idea that you could save yourself by placing less value on the life of an Arab than on that of a white man seemed as dishonest to me as it would have done to Meursault. The discovery that such a subversive book was published in France under the noses of the occupying forces in 1942 was the icing on the cake; the German censor found nothing objectionable about it, apparently.

Camus himself was just what a bookish 15-year-old was looking for in a literary hero. Amis, Braine, Wilson & Co all seemed terribly provincial and looked like schoolmasters. In spite of all the drugs and jazz and beards, the American lot were too much in thrall to the windy excesses of Walt Whitman, who didn't seem to have much to do with the twentieth century. Camus had actually done something, not least edited a resistance newspaper during the occupation. A stubbly Frenchman with a Boyard dangling from the corner of his mouth fitted in perfectly with my notion of what a writer ought to be; he belonged with all those other stubbly Frenchmen – Belmondo, Gainsbourg, Sartre and so on – whose toad-like visages seemed not to get in the way of a busy love-life.

While I waited to get stubbly enough I practised mumbling enigmatically with a No. 6 in the corner of my mouth, squinting through the smoke. (Eventually, of course, I cottoned on to the fact that they all, particularly Camus, wanted to look like Humphrey Bogart, and that his unadorned prose came straight from such hard-boiled luminaries as James M. Cain and Dashiell Hammett.) The manner of Camus's death in 1960 seemed all of a piece with his dangerous allure. To smash against a tree in a Facel Vega, the most glamorous of all French cars, his publisher at the wheel, was the apotheosis of the Absurd. Ah yes, the Absurd . . .

If truth be told, I never quite got the hang of Existentialism. 'Existence precedes Essence,' I would say to myself solemnly, and then go off to the youth club to play table tennis. *The Outsider* appealed to me on a much more visceral level than mere philosophy; it seemed to be about *me*, and I wasn't interested in constructing general principles around the unique being that was *moi*. Such ridiculous solipsism didn't last long – the Beatles' first LP was on the horizon, after all, and everything was about to be different. I quickly learned in any case that girls didn't respond well to the proposition that if they really wanted to understand me they should read *The Outsider*. Meanwhile my mother bore the fact that I was trying out being stolid in the event of her death with her usual forbearance.

Rereading the book recently (and how many of Professor Jardine's 400 can say that, I wonder?), I was pleased to find that *The Outsider* still makes a spare and effective fable. Its unadorned prose carries no period baggage or local colour; you would never know that it was set in North Africa, in fact. True, there are Arabs; one gets murdered, after all. But a similar novel set in contemporary France might well feature Arabs in exactly the same way. The heat, the dust, the beaches, the *piscines*, the pompous might of the state, all seem more than adequately French.

In his condemned cell Meursault rejoices in the benign indifference of the universe; at a time when the universe begins to seem less indifferent and certainly less benign, this might appear perverse. If we are killing the planet because we can't be bothered not to, then *The Outsider* is a fitting text to accompany its demise. You can't say *that* about *The Hobbit*.

MIKE PETTY conducts his existence as Publishing Manager of the Eden Project in Cornwall, and tries to restrain his dealings with essence to the kitchen.

Ibn Battutah Meets Forrest Gump

JUSTIN MAROZZI

In the Spring edition of *Slightly Foxed*, Paul Routledge defied anyone to read Fitzroy Maclean's *Eastern Approaches* and not want to head off at once to Central Asia. I think he is absolutely right about that. A little later in his essay, he writes, 'If there is a more romantic opening to a book, not just a travel book but any book, then I don't know of it.' I think he is wrong about that. Or perhaps, which is quite probable, he has not come across the Lebanese writer Amin Maalouf's *Leo the African*, whose opening sentences I read as an impressionable 18-year-old on the verge of my first visit to Cairo.

> I, Hasan the son of Muhammad the weigh-master, I, Jean-Leon de Medici, circumcised at the hand of a barber and baptized at the hand of a pope, I am now called the African, but I am not from Africa, nor from Europe, nor from Arabia. I am also called the Granadan, the Fasi, the Zayyati, but I come from no country, from no city, no tribe. I am the son of the road, my country is the caravan, my life the most unexpected of voyages.

By the second paragraph, I was completely lost to the Middle East. Who wouldn't be?

> My wrists have experienced in turn the caresses of silk, the abuses of wool, the gold of princes and the chains of slaves. My

---

Amin Maalouf, *Leo the African* (1988) · Translated by Peter Sluglett
Abacus · Pb · 360pp · £8.99 · ISBN 0349106002

fingers have parted a thousand veils, my lips have made a thousand virgins blush, and my eyes have seen cities die and empires perish.

Perhaps I was particularly receptive to this romanticized view of the Arab world. My father was born in Beirut in 1938, grew up in Aleppo, Damascus, Jerusalem and Cairo, and spent much of his adult life doing business in North Africa and the Middle East. Libyans, Iraqis and Pakistanis kept popping up in our family home throughout my childhood before being whisked off to Liberty's and Laura Ashley by my father to shop for presents for their wives and children. I remember my mother fielding questions as to whether the meat was *halal* – often it wasn't – and on one occasion disapproving of my father taking some sort of treatment for impotence to a friend in Tripoli. There were always a lot of kaftans and *jalabiyas* in the house.

It was only after reading a number of novels by Naguib Mahfouz, who won the Nobel Prize for Literature in 1988, the same year *Leo the African* first appeared in English, that I discovered Amin Maalouf's wonderful picaresque novel. This was to be the first stage in a curiously circular path that led to North Africa and thence, for a book I was writing on Libya, to the real-life Leo Africanus, the sixteenth-century traveller, diplomat and writer on whose extraordinary career the novel is based.

The life of Leo, or Hassan al-Wazzan, as he is also known, is itself rich in romance. Born a Muslim in Granada, Leo accompanied his family into exile in Fez shortly after Ferdinand and Isabella's conquest of the last Muslim stronghold in Spain in 1492. As a young man he travelled extensively across North Africa, through the Sahara and further south into the Niger Basin on several diplomatic missions, before being captured by Barbary corsairs near the island of Jerba in around 1520. He was then presented to Pope Leo X as a gift, an educated and highly travelled ornament for the papal court. His probably tactical conversion to Christianity soon after his arrival inspired the pope to free him from slavery, allowing Leo free rein to continue his studies and write his evocative *Description of Africa*, published in 1526. His later years are shrouded in mystery but it is thought he left Rome shortly before its sacking in 1527 – Maalouf has him there as an eyewitness for dramatic effect – and, after further travels north of the Mediterranean, returned to North Africa where he died in about 1550.

So there he is, East meets West in one man, a window on the fall of Granada and the Spanish Inquisition, the Ottoman conquest of Egypt, and Renaissance Rome under the Medicis. Maalouf's novel sparkles with life, conjuring up the sights, smells and sounds of the great Arab cities – from the opulence of palace life to the terrors of a leper colony – and the tension of an embattled Rome encircled by a Lutheran mob. The prose is rich and graceful, and the English-language edition is beautifully translated by Peter Sluglett.

Tragedies, scandals, good fortune and reversals come and go. The political is always threatening to overwhelm the personal, but our itinerant scholarly hero refuses to be overcome by the succession of storms that break over him. He makes and loses fortunes, cheats murderous bandits, is banished for a crime he didn't commit, picks up a sword and goes to war, adopts a child destined to become the Ottoman sultan, performs the *haj* to Mecca, and so it goes on. *Leo the African* recalls the mesmerizing density of adventure in *Don Quixote* and *Candide*, though its protagonist is more thoughtful – part Ibn Battutah, part Forrest Gump, an enlightened, multilingual man of many cultures.

'From my mouth you will hear Arabic, Turkish, Castilian, Berber, Hebrew, Latin and vulgar Italian, because all tongues and all prayers belong to me,' he says at the outset. 'But I belong to none of them. I belong only to God and to the earth, and it is to them that I will one day soon return.'

During the course of his travels, Leo meets the great and the good of his era. He is befriended by the Moroccan sultan in Fez, has an audience with Barbarossa, welcomes Tumanbay, last of the Mamluk sultans, to his home, appears before Sultan Selim the Grim on a diplomatic mission to Constantinople, and is baptized by Pope Leo X in the Eternal City.

Diplomacy takes up much of his energies but he manages always to find time to indulge the affairs of the heart. He embarks on several love affairs. Some bring happiness, others are doomed to disappear in the dust of the Sahara. One of his greatest loves is his first, a 14-year-old slave girl called Hiba whom he keeps for several years. 'My only home was in her eyes, her lips, her hands,' he says, but they are separated when he gives her back her freedom deep in the desert in return for an impromptu act of generosity which saves him from ruin. In Cairo he falls for Nur, a beautiful Circassian woman with a dangerous secret, a young son whom she intends for the Ottoman throne. They, too, are separated after he is abducted from the beach one night by pirates and taken into captivity. Then in Rome he is matched with Maddalena, a one-time convent girl who steals his heart for ever.

Maalouf writes movingly and from bitter personal experience about exile, war, ethnic tensions and the problems of cultural identity. In 1975, after civil war broke out, he exchanged Lebanon for Paris. There are times in the novel when Leo is fleeing danger with a wife and young children in tow. The passages have a fear and immediacy about them which come, in part, from the time when Maalouf and his pregnant wife and small son huddled together in their basement in Beirut as all around outside gunmen fought in the streets. Leo's life is a constant form of exile, sometimes voluntary, more often forced upon him by political events beyond his control. Nostalgia and resignation pervade the prose.

Rereading *Leo* after almost twenty years, I find Maalouf's vision of tolerance between different cultures, above all between East and West, all the more striking in an age dominated by an unfathomable war on terror. *Leo the African* ends with a heartfelt piece of advice from Leo to his son as the boat on which he is writing these memoirs nears the North African coast. His own wanderings, he says, have come to an end. His gait is heavy, his breathing burdensome. His only desire now is to spend the rest of his life peacefully in the bosom of his family. He cautions his son to watch out for those who, later in life, will surely question his identity.

> Wherever you are, some will want to ask you questions about your skin or your prayers. Beware of gratifying their instincts, my son, beware of bending before the multitude! Muslim, Jew or Christian, they must take you as you are, or lose you. When men's minds seem narrow to you, tell yourself that the land of God is broad; broad His hands and broad His heart. Never hesitate to go far away, beyond all seas, all frontiers, all countries, all beliefs.

JUSTIN MAROZZI travelled across Libya on a camel and has just finished *Islamistan*, a hard-hitting satire on Iraq. Who's going to publish it? Answers, please, to jsmarozzi@aol.com before he publishes it himself in Baghdad.

A Notorious Baggage

ROGER HUDSON

We can touch the past through diaries, letters and memoirs, which allow a measure of intimacy and immediacy even across the centuries. The accepted view is that they begin to proliferate in the second half of the seventeenth century with Pepys, Evelyn, Lucy Hutchinson and John Aubrey. But there is an earlier figure who has somehow slipped below the literary horizon. The letters that John Chamberlain (1554–1628) wrote are the first in English that can be read without difficulty and with pleasure.

Chamberlain was well placed to be an observer of the end of Elizabeth's reign and the subsequent Jacobean period. His father had been Master of the Ironmongers' Company in London, as were three of his brothers. His was therefore a comfortably off family, on the cusp between the urban middle class and the gentry. He went to Trinity, Cambridge, but did not take a degree; attended Gray's Inn, but was not called to the bar; never had a job and never married. He knew his station and his limitations: 'I never did abound, so I was . . . never in want . . . I am past all ambition and wish nor seek nothing but how to live *suaviter* and in plenty.' Here was an ideal looker-on, gathering all the news and gossip in circulation on his daily visits to St Paul's Cathedral where he and many others went 'Paul's Walking', up and down its naves and aisles. By far the greatest number of his letters are to Dudley Carleton, a career diplomat much

---

A number of copies of Elizabeth Thomson's one-volume selection (John Murray, 1966) of her father N. E. McClure's two-volume edition of *The Chamberlain Letters* (1939) can be found on various Internet book sites.

younger than he who is anxious to be kept abreast of what is happening back in England.

This is the age of Shakespeare, though alas Chamberlain makes no mention of him. He does, however, report the burning of the Globe Theatre in 1613 after its thatched roof was set alight by the discharge of a stage cannon, and of the Fortune Theatre in 1621, owned by Edward Alleyn, the founder of Dulwich College. He also gives frequent evidence of how the English language had suddenly caught fire, not merely at the hands of the playwrights and poets of the period, but also among ordinary men of the middling sort, such as himself. Right from the earliest letters in the 1590s phrases flash out on the page. He says the treasurer of the Earl of Essex's expedition to Ireland 'shall not be troubled with much receipt . . . a well saddled rat may carry all his accounts'. He is all too prophetic and the following year (1598) talks of Ireland being 'farther out of square than ever, so that there is no other way but to provide the sharper sword'.

It is this combination of historical and literary appeal that should earn Chamberlain a much wider audience. In 1601 he is present at the trial of Essex for treason: 'I never saw any go through with such boldness and show of resolution and contempt of death; but whether this courage were borrowed and put on for the time, or natural, it is hard to judge.' Essex was doomed, 'Yet the general opinion is there will be no great executions, for the Queen is very gracious and inclines much to mercy.' Throughout the letters it is the King (or Queen), Princes, Princesses and royal favourites who, as the motive forces of society, dominate proceedings. Chamberlain makes this plain, confessing in December 1616 that 'The King's and Queen's absence, together with the end of the [law] term, hath made this town as barren of news as it is of good company.'

The high (or low) points in these years are the Catholics' attempt to blow up James in 1605, the death of his eldest son Henry in 1612, the marriage of his daughter Elizabeth, the Winter Queen, to the Rhineland ruler, the Elector Palatine, in 1613, and the attempted

'Spanish Match' of his son Charles followed by his successful marriage to Henrietta Maria of France.

Guy Fawkes is 'taken, making his trains at midnight with a blind lantern'. To the physicians, 'the extremity of Prince Henry's disease seemed to lie in his head, for remedy whereof they shaved him and applied warm cocks and pigeons newly killed, but with no success'. A week after his death 'a very handsome young fellow . . . came stark naked to St James's while they were at supper, saying he was the Prince's ghost come from heaven with a message for the King . . . All the penance they gave him was two or three lashes, which he endured as it seemed without sense, and keeping him naked as he was all night and the next day in the porter's lodge, where thousands came to see him.' The morning after the marriage of 'the Palsgrave and the Lady Elizabeth . . . the King went to visit these young turtles that were coupled on St Valentine's Day, and did strictly examine him whether he were his true son-in-law, and was sufficiently assured'. When the English party return from the unsuccessful attempt to marry Charles to the Spanish Infanta, they report finding 'nothing but penury and proud beggary, besides all other discourtesy', in her country. Then in December 1624, 'We had here great triumph and rejoicing for the good forwardness of the French match, by public commandment: the organs in Paul's played two hours on their loudest pipes, and so began to the bells, the bells to the bonfires, the bonfires to a great peal of ordnance at the Tower. God grant it may prove worth all this noise.'

In December 1614 Chamberlain grumbles that 'For all this penurious world, we speak of a masque this Christmas towards which the King gives £1,500, the principal motive whereof is thought to be the gracing of Young Villiers [James's new favourite, the future Duke of Buckingham] and to bring him on the stage.' The royal finances were always in a parlous state in spite of subterfuges such as the sale of the new rank of baronet, invented in 1611, for about £1,000 each, or the making of 50 new barons at £6,000 each, suggested in 1615 – 'I think

'A notorious baggage':
Moll Cut-purse

they should scant have found five at that rate.' In addition, 'new gifts and daily warrants under the privy signet do alter the course of orderly payments and disorder all', as did the irresponsible granting of monopolies to courtiers. The 'new plantations of Virginia and Bermuda are like to be stifled as it were in the cradle' by a tobacco monopoly granted in 1620, and there are others: 'for scouring and trimming of armour throughout England; . . . for sixpence a load of hay of all that comes to this town by land or water; . . . for whatsoever is printed but on one side'.

Chamberlain could not see 'how the King's wants can be supplied', except by 'the ordinary, ancient, and plain highway' of taxation authorized by Parliament. The trouble was that 'Impositions and patents [monopolies] are grown so grievous that of necessity they must be spoken of [by the Commons], and the prerogative [the King's 'divine right' to them], on the other side, is become so tender that it cannot endure to be touched.' Here we see perhaps the largest of the seeds which were to grow into the Civil War two decades later.

There is plenty of illuminating trivia to counterbalance such high matters of state. In 1601, 'Last week one came hopping from Charing Cross into Paul's bound in a sack, and another carried up a horse and rode upon him to the top of Paul's steeple.' In 1605, 'Dr Milward, preaching at Paul's Cross, a cuckoo came flying over the pulpit and very lewdly called and cried out.' In 1612, 'Moll Cut-purse, a notorious baggage (that used to go in man's apparel and challenged the field of diverse gallants), was brought to Paul's Cross, where she wept bitterly and seemed very penitent, but it is since doubted [for] she was maudlin drunk, being discovered to have tippled off three quarts of sack before she came to her penance.' Six years later, 'Mistress West, the Lord Delaware's daughter, one of our prime and principal beauties, is seized on by the smallpox, which if they [the pox marks] deal not mercifully with her she is quite undone, seeing her good face is the best part of her fortune.' In 1619, 'A woman of Whitefriars held her maid's head so long in a tub of water, that she drowned her. And a player about the town, upon some displeasure to the Lord of Doncaster's barber (that was very dear to him), ran him through and killed him unawares.'

Much of this may seem far removed from life today, but then one comes on an item that suddenly concertinas the intervening centuries: 'We have every week almost a new proclamation for somewhat or other, as for buildings (forward and backward), for weights and measures, for inns and alehouses, for horse meat, and I know not what else, all for the good of the subject, and yet they either believe it not or will not acknowledge the good pretended.' John Chamberlain is one of us.

ROGER HUDSON's modestly titled *Hudson's English History* came out last autumn, when his anthology drawn from letters and diaries and called *Murray's Daily Companion* also appeared.

Escape Routes

AMANDA THEUNISSEN

I once interviewed a well-known poet on the radio and asked him what he read when he had 'flu. He looked at me with astonishment – and some contempt – and said 'Tolstoy, of course'. But when I have 'flu I don't reach for the classics, I reach for *Modesty Blaise*.

She and her lethal associate and friend, Willie Garvin, started life in 1963 as a strip cartoon in London's *Evening Standard*, and went on to star in a series of inventive thrillers by Peter O'Donnell, who created the original cartoon with the artist Jim Holdaway. I started to read them at least thirty years ago and I was hooked straight away. Modesty Blaise was the first of the strong, feisty women – Emma Peel's elder sister or Charlie's Angel's aunt. Unlike them, however, she's not working for any male mastermind. She only does what she wants, and if that involves going outside the law, that's fine.

As a young mother in the '60s who'd been brought up in English boarding schools and was trying hard to escape their clammy embrace, I felt she was everything I wanted to be: a retired criminal

---

Peter O'Donnell, *Modesty Blaise* (1965) · 224pp · ISBN 0285637282; *Sabre Tooth* (1966) · 288pp · ISBN 0285636766; *I Lucifer* (1967) · 320pp · ISBN 028563707X; *A Taste for Death* (1969) · 288pp · ISBN 0285637657; *Impossible Virgin* (1971) · 288pp · ISBN 0285636146; *Silver Mistress* (1973) · 256pp · ISBN 0285636448; *Last Day in Limbo* (1976) · 256pp · ISBN 0285636758; *Dragon's Claw* (1978) · 272pp · ISBN 0285637088; *Xanadu Talisman* (1981) · 288pp · ISBN 028563643X; *Night of the Morningstar* (1982) · 288pp · ISBN 0285636154; *Dead Man's Handle* (1985) · 240pp · ISBN 0285637274; *Cobra Trap* (1996) · 288pp · ISBN 0285637665; all published in paperback by Souvenir Press at £8.99.

who ran an international gang from the age of 17, and incredibly rich – she and Willie are only tempted out of retirement to do dangerous and secret jobs for the British government, involving colourful villains who want to take over the world or make a lot of money.

She is very beautiful, of course, with long legs, a long neck and 'skin a matt brown that would make a fortune for the man who could bottle it'. She also has big midnight-blue eyes that go black when she's fighting for her life. Which happens all the time.

She can shoot with deadly accuracy and fight to win in all kinds of unarmed combat (never beaten except when her opponent cheats by using ESP). She can swim, fence, dive, hang-glide, dance, speak many languages, and she's a mistress of disguise. She has an internal compass and clock that tell her where she is and what the time is anywhere in the world, and she can live off the land. She has total muscle control. She can put herself into a trance at will (as a young mother I longed to be able to do that). She can run backwards as fast as forwards, fighting at the same time. Oh, and go to the lavatory while in handcuffs – definitely an unusual social skill.

And another great thing about her is that although she's very feminine she doesn't do the dreary domestic stuff. A bit of cooking, yes; washing up, cleaning, shopping, ironing, laundry, putting the bins out, definitely no. Not surprisingly, given all that, men adore her but she has only two women friends – one a blind psychic Canadian and the other a Scottish earl's daughter with one leg. Not a lot of competition there.

She doesn't work for men, they work for her. She sleeps with whoever she likes, but never the incomparable Cockney charmer, Willie Garvin. Who wouldn't want a Willie Garvin by their side? He's her best friend and he's not even gay. Tall, strong, brave and good-looking, raised in an orphanage and an approved school, he spent a lot of time in prison before being found by Modesty in a Thai jail and released to a new life. 'They tell me you are a dangerous rat, Willie Garvin. I've no use for rats but I've got a hunch there's some sort of man inside you trying to get out. If you work for me, he might get a chance.'

Willie worships the ground his Princess (as he calls her) walks on, and their relationship is based on total understanding and trust. They do everything together – except have sex. As Modesty explains to one baffled lover, '"We've got stronger bonds than that. We've worked together, fought together, saved each other's lives. We've had a fair taste of hell together, we've been hurt, we've nursed each other and we've won together. Everything but this." She laid her hand on the bed.' It's a perfect friendship that binds all the books together until the very end.

You can tell they first appeared as a strip cartoon. It's a two-dimensional world and – it's got to be said – a bit silly. I think that's fine, in fact the sillier the better. That's what escapism's about. Perhaps because of a cartoon's need for action and a cliff-hanger in four frames every day, six days a week, things move extremely fast. Every page brings new action – most of it gloriously beyond the edge of probability.

It's difficult to choose a favourite scene. I'm very fond of the one in *Dragon's Claw* where Modesty, sailing alone across the Tasman Sea, runs into a storm, a great white shark and an unconscious man in a rubber dingy simultaneously. And manages to swim out to the dingy, hoist the man on board and fight off the shark with a broom handle. All single-handed. Or maybe when, in *Xanadu Talisman*, Willie saves them both by lassoing a black panther with just the nylon thread from his trousers. But what about Modesty's escape from the gorilla's cage or Willie surviving being thrown out of an aeroplane at 18,000 feet strapped to his seat (*The Impossible Virgin*), or the battle with the murderous Siamese twins in a remote Himalayan valley (*Sabre Tooth*)?

In a piece he wrote for the *Crime Time* website, Peter O'Donnell says he based Modesty on a strange meeting he had in 1942 with a refugee in the Iranian desert. One day 'a small figure appeared wearing a thin unbleached shirt that fell to just below her knees. On her head she carried a small bundle wrapped in a piece of blanket, and something hung on her chest from a cord looped about her neck.' The 'something' turned out to be a crude weapon – 'I felt chilled as I wondered what might have brought home to her the need for some way of defending herself.'

He and his companions gave her food and a tin opener: 'That was when she smiled, and to me it seemed you could've lit up a small village with that smile. We watched as she put the bundle on her head and walked away. To this day I can see in my mind's eye the smile she had given us and the sight of that upright little figure walking like a princess on those brave skinny legs.'

To fill in Modesty's background, O'Donnell gave her a childhood companion, a brilliant, highly educated, 50-year-old Jewish professor called Lob who spoke five languages and taught her everything he knew as they wandered around the Middle East. When he died she went off to run a criminal gang, The Network, in Tangier. That was her education. Even now it seems to me to be more fun than boarding school.

The Modesty Blaise books belong firmly to the cultural context of the '60s and early '70s. There are no computers or mobiles. Instead we get terrible music and nylon clothes, and everyone smokes all the time. When Modesty retires from crime she has amassed £500,000, which in those days was real money, enough to live on for ever, allowing her to concentrate on doing what she likes best – fighting villains with Willie. Often she gets sent off on these capers by the slightly creepy Sir Gerard Talent, who runs some shadowy security department. He's clearly meant to be Modesty's father figure but he seems to spend a lot of time admiring the curves of her bosom under her thin silk shirt. Not to mention greasing her naked body with engine oil in some underground cave before a fight with yet another villain – that never sounded very fatherly to me.

However criminal they may appear, Modesty and Willie are always on the side of the angels. They have their own code, which they never break. They kill a lot of people but only those who deserve it. The rich cast of baddies kill, trap, torture and generally show total disregard for the finer things in life. And the conclusions are just as they should be: the bad guys lose in the end and the good guys pay enough of a price for their victories to keep the tension going. This lack of moral uncertainty makes for good escapism. After all, who wants to be troubled with difficult ethical issues in fantasy land?

I can quite see that the poet would never even pick up one of these books, which is a shame. It's impossible to live on the high ground all the time, and energetic, action-packed, nylon-clad romps like these are hard to find. There are thirteen in the series – all but one currently in print – starting with *Modesty Blaise* and ending, in every sense, with *Cobra Trap*. Just think, 'flu need never be boring again. In fact, I think I may have to lie down and do some rereading.

AMANDA THEUNISSEN is a television producer who worked for the BBC for 20 years, making high-minded and intellectually testing programmes at a time when that was acceptable. She was often a guest on BBC Radio book programmes but, in spite of that, is badly read in the classics – though she can bluff her way through most occasions. She has an insatiable appetite for schlock.

The cartoons themselves, from which the image on p.28 is taken, are published by Triton Books.

The Unobtrusive Gardener

URSULA BUCHAN

I had just come home from a protracted springtime tour of English gardens. Perhaps it was their ravishing fresh beauty, or their complexity, or their immaculate neatness, or perhaps I had just seen one topiary box spiral too many. Most likely, it was the stark impossibility of ever achieving in my garden anything approaching the quality I had seen elsewhere. Whatever the reason, a light melancholy descended on me, like a thin summer rain. I went deliberately to the bookshelf and took down a book which I had not read since it was first published in 1997. I needed a dose of Geoffrey Dutton – poet, gardener, professor of medical science, white-water swimmer and mountaineer – to help me regain my usual cheery equilibrium.

Some Branch Against the Sky is a book about the nine acres of the Scottish Highlands in Perthshire where Geoffrey Dutton had gardened 'marginally' for forty years by the time the book was published. I hope he does so still. I turned to it because his experiences of making a congruous garden on acid soil in a wild gorge in the hills are so very different from my own on alkaline clay in the rolling lowlands of rural Northamptonshire, and his furrow, so to speak, is so much harder to plough. And also because he is one of the few writers who makes gardening and all its penumbra of weather, soil, light, shade, blossoming and withering, success and failure, both absorbing and revealing.

Geoffrey Dutton, *Some Branch Against the Sky: The Practice and Principles of Marginal Gardening* (1997), is now out of print but copies can be obtained via the Internet or through second-hand bookshops.

The hardest task for any gardening writer is to describe convincingly, and attractively, a garden, whether it is their own or someone else's. Too often, garden descriptions degenerate into bald directions of the 'Turn left at the fish pond' variety. Atmosphere is so important to a garden, yet so elusive to conjure. The best gardening writers, like the best cricket writers, say, can explain what it is like to be there. In this book, Geoffrey Dutton first describes the garden, with good maps as an accompaniment, and then settles down to tell the reader what it is like to be there at all four seasons of the year.

What Geoffrey Dutton calls 'marginal' gardening is looking after a place of obviously great natural beauty and drama, and intervening, horticulturally, as little and as carefully as is consistent with a desire to grow those exotic plants, such as rhododendrons, which happily settle into such an environment and don't look out of place in it. As he puts it:

> Gardening here can be termed marginal for two main reasons. First because of the soil and climate. Second because the site was already attractive: a tumble of birch and juniper scrub, heather moor and a moss-hung thundering gorge. Any gardening therefore had to be unobtrusive: a guiding of the latent design, a prolonged consultation with the Genius of the Place. Intensive horticulture would ruin it.

Would that more gardeners were so sensitive.

Open the book anywhere at random and you will read a striking, memorable phrase or paragraph:

> The path climbs to the next constriction, brushes through hemlock sprays and the stiffer protests of *Abies procera*, and turns left. It uncovers a prospect at which the 18th-century devotees of the Sublime might have fluttered their canes in approval.

He is particularly good on cold (the temperature regularly going below -15° C in winter) and the many types of snow:

> All is now hushed. Feet crump on dry powder. The silence is an insulation from, not an absence of, noise. There is a constant background hiss as airy cakes release themselves from branchwork, the slow following clouds of dust puffing against black trunks . . .
>
> I remember one morning in Coille Dubh [a part of the garden] when a great number of trees had been shattered [by snow], and others were here and there exploding with sharp reports in the stillness (for trees burst under stress). The air was acrid with birch-juice. Huge hanging chandeliers of ice, dizzy glaciers rotating far above your head, menaced progress. Light slanted through strange new spaces and snow-hung wreckage. It was dawn after an air raid. Landmarks had gone, those lichened columns known and patted for years; no familiar space-measurers, no eye-intervals, were left. And as it was April, birdsong thrilled through the devastation. Yet I recall such things with a kind of pleasure, looking at a changed Coille Dubh equally attractive now in its new right.

His observational powers are impressive, his knowledge of the kind of plants which will both survive in such unusual and trying circumstances and look fitting in the context, is exceptional, and he has the grace to recognize that he is only one of a number of creatures that inhabit such a glorious place. He was plainly an ecologist before we all knew the term. Best of all, he has both a broad hinterland and an understated, but piquant, sense of humour.

Geoffrey Dutton (known in the world of published poetry as G.F. Dutton, in order to differentiate him, I imagine, from the Australian writer of the same name) has a number of books of poetry to his name, such as *Camp One* and *The Concrete Garden*, as well as ones on mountaineering and wild-water swimming (there is a natural swimming pool at the top of his sloping garden before the stream plunges into the gorge). However, he made his name with keen gardeners when he wrote a series of articles on his garden for *The Garden*, the journal of the Royal Horticultural Society, between 1988 and 1994. These, together with forty years of daily diary jottings, form the basis of the book.

There seems to me only one aspect which disappoints, even slightly. Although the descriptions of the topography and plant life in the book are extremely clear and precise, they are not helped by the accompanying monochrome pictures. Some, such as one of the burn in the gorge, are dramatic, but too many are just a jumble of trees of indeterminate species. Considering what a remarkable and, I think one can assume, successful garden this is (and one which I do not believe is open to the public) this is a pity. Notwithstanding, this is a gardening book for all those allergic to the 'plant it, prune it, feed it, let me make you feel guilty and inadequate' school of horticultural literature. Take it from me, *Some Branch Against the Sky* is a dependable cure for mild melancholia.

URSULA BUCHAN is a gardening writer and journalist who has a country garden in Northamptonshire, which is sometimes gardened rather marginally, but not in the way Geoffrey Dutton uses the term.

The Road to Room 101

GORDON BOWKER

Every time I go into one of those old-fashioned second-hand bookshops – the ones with rows of leather-bound copies of *Punch* and shelves full of long-expired novels and the sweet smell of decaying paper pervading the air – I think of Gordon Comstock, George Orwell's anti-hero in *Keep the Aspidistra Flying*. Poor Gordon, an advertising dropout and aspiring poet who is scraping a living as an assistant in such a bookshop, is forever bemoaning a world ruled by 'the Money God' rather than the Muses.

Keep the Aspidistra Flying is Orwell's most autobiographical novel, written in 1935, when temporarily his career appeared to have stalled. His first two books, *Down and Out in Paris and London* and *Burmese Days*, had earned him some modest critical acclaim, but his second novel, *A Clergyman's Daughter*, had had a mixed reception. It had been written under the influence of James Joyce's *Ulysses* and had been part-experimental, but the experiment had failed. So he jettisoned the ambition to write highly poetic fiction and at the same time abandoned any lingering hope of ever shining as a poet. Henceforth his prose would be pared down and economical, aspiring to an ideal of clarity – the clarity, he said, of a windowpane.

Since the end of 1934, he had been living in Hampstead, working part-time, like Gordon, for a bookseller. A job among mostly forgotten books seemed to symbolize what he then saw as his own failure as a writer. He was also frustrated in love. Too poor to get married,

---

George Orwell, *Keep the Aspidistra Flying* (1936)
Penguin · Pb · 288pp · £8.99 · ISBN 0141183721

he was reduced to occasional affairs with 'liberated' girlfriends or encounters with prostitutes. He had a lot to get out of his system, and his anger and frustration would soon be channelled into his own brand of left-wing politics. By the end of the year he had met his future wife and was about to set foot on 'the road to Wigan Pier' to study the effects of mass unemployment in the industrial north, a journey towards socialism which became eventually the road to *Animal Farm* and *Nineteen Eighty-Four*.

When I first read *Keep the Aspidistra Flying* in my teens, I didn't think much of it. The London it conjured up was a grim one, a cold, colourless world of dingy boarding-houses, soulless drudgery, unfulfilled ambition, frustrated sexuality and unyielding snobbery. An obsession with money and scraping around for the price of a meal or a packet of fags is a recurrent motif. Here is Orwell at his most resentful and unforgiving, hating a society peopled by vainglorious poets, back-scratching critics, posing book collectors and dishonest advertisers. Gordon, his doppelgänger, is at war with the whole social set-up, and especially the cosy world of respectability into which he feels his girlfriend Rosemary is attempting to lure him, a dismal world symbolized by the omnipresent aspidistra.

Many of the novel's ingredients are drawn directly from his experiences at the time he was writing it – most notably the dreary routine of the bookshop, its eccentric customers, his relationships with girlfriends, his friendship with Sir Richard Rees (the aristocratic literary editor who bailed him out from time to time), and his self-mortifying excursions into the underworld of the Lambeth slums, where not long before he had dossed among the down-and-outs. He was still anxious to purge himself of the burden of sin he felt he had incurred as a young imperial policeman in Burma, and degradation and poverty, he thought, were the way to free himself of the guilt.

> He wanted to go down, deep down, into some world where decency no longer mattered; to cut the strings of his self-

> respect, to submerge himself – to sink . . . It was all bound up in his mind with the thought of being underground. He liked to think about the lost people, the underground people, tramps, beggars, criminals, prostitutes. It is a good world that they inhabit, down there in their frowzy kips and spikes. He liked to think that beneath the world of money there is that great sluttish underworld where failure and success have no meaning; a sort of kingdom of ghosts where all are equal. That was where he wished to be, down in the ghost-kingdom, below ambition.

Orwell's conscience was always hard at work in anything he wrote. In all his novels – from *Burmese Days*, which drew on those experiences as a policeman, to *Nineteen Eighty-Four* – Paradise is first gained and then lost. Here, for Gordon, the Paradise of being an occasionally published poet, living free from bourgeois respectability and the Money God in squalid South London digs, is lost when he is trapped (by Rosemary's pregnancy) into marriage, a respectable job back in advertising, and a house in the suburbs with, of course, the dreaded aspidistra conspicuously on display.

Literary biographers are often warned not to seek their subjects in their works of fiction, but Orwell believed that we could best glimpse the inner world of an author through his creative writing, and *Keep the Aspidistra Flying* contains many elements through which we can read his character and enter into the consciousness of a man on the brink of a great writing career. After it was published, because of tuberculosis, he had less than fifteen years to live, and here as in all his novels there are clocks throughout chiming and ticking away the minutes of any remaining life. While completing the novel, Orwell had decided, like Gordon, that he was not after all a poet, and he wrote almost no verse thereafter; he was also determined, like Gordon, to live in virtual poverty to be able to write freely rather than to order; he did, like Gordon, refuse his family's blandishments to find a 'good job', and he did finally settle for marriage – though not because he had to – and retreated to a house, not in the suburbs, however, but in the countryside, far removed from aspidistras.

Although it attracted a fan letter from the young Anthony Powell and words of appreciation from Edith Sitwell, the novel was panned by his friends Cyril Connolly and Richard Rees, who disliked its prevailing air of squalor and what Rees called its 'loose violence of style'. Because in its first draft it had included some mild swear-words, the names of well-known businesses (Drages and the Times Furnishing Company among them) and slighting comments about the popular novelists Ethel M. Dell and Warwick Deeping, Victor Gollancz, his publisher, ever-fearful of libel actions, demanded cuts. Orwell later complained that the *Aspidistra* had been mangled by lawyers, and he came to dismiss it as a pot-boiler, written solely for money. It was one of the few of his books he left instructions was not to be reprinted, and for years he never even owned a copy.

George Orwell, by Mark Handley

However, Orwell did manage to slip in a couple of jokes that evaded the attention of both publisher and lawyers. One is a poem that Gordon recites to Rosemary in a moment of lustful passion. It's in medieval French which, when translated, proves to be a sly invitation to a pornographic act. The joke is only intensified by the name of his protagonist – Comstock was the name of the founder of the New York Society for the Suppression of Vice, and 'Comstockery', of course, had come to mean an unjustified excess of prudery. Having Gordon utter these words, therefore, was a delightfully subtle protest against those who would have cut his book even more had they had the wit to understand what he was up to.

Preparing a biography of Orwell, naturally I reread all his work, but I did not approach *Keep the Aspidistra Flying* with any great sense of excitement. However, just before reading it again, I saw the film of the novel, dramatized by Alan Plater and starring Richard E. Grant as the angry young poet. It quite transformed my reading of the book. What in my youth I had read as a bleak tale of failure I now saw as an exuberant satire of 1930s literary London, revealing a little-known Rabelaisian side of Orwell. The gloomy anti-hero, Gordon, had somehow transformed himself into a brilliantly comic character, a forerunner of John Osborne's Jimmy Porter, and the scourge not only of corrupt book reviewers and posturing poets but of the whole money culture in general.

Then, too, it became clear that it occupied an important place in Orwell's creative oeuvre. His friend Julian Symons was probably the first to notice a connection between his first novel, *Burmese Days*, and his last, *Nineteen Eighty-Four*, with each of his intervening novels working towards that final great work. Gordon Comstock is brother to John Flory of *Burmese Days*, and George Bowling of *Coming Up for Air*, as well as Winston Smith of *Nineteen Eighty-Four*.

Gordon is conducting a private underground war against the Money God, just as Winston is secretly plotting to bring down Big Brother. He is spied on by his landlady, Mrs Wisbech, just as Winston is spied on by his neighbours, the Parsons family and the Thought Police. He lusts after his fiancée Rosemary just as Winston lusts after Julia, the girl from the Fiction Department of the Ministry of Truth, and both consummate their relationships in an idyllic country setting. Finally, having tasted a false freedom in the slums of Lambeth, Gordon is defeated, embracing the respectability he had previously despised and becoming the proud owner of the dreaded aspidistra, while Winston, having also found a haven among the proles and imagining himself to be free, succumbs finally to the tortures of Room 101 and finds himself loving Big Brother.

This is one of those books – some of George Gissing's novels about Grub Street fall into the same category – that can suddenly acquire a new significance in a new age, and beckon us to look at it afresh. The times, one might say, have ensured that *Keep the Aspidistra Flying* flies again.

GORDON BOWKER first discovered Orwell while working among books – not in a bookshop, but in a library. He blames him for having been lured, for a time, away from Literature into Sociology, but has long since forgiven him. He has, at least, managed to avoid the Orwellian nightmare of exile to suburbia. Aspidistras, he is pleased to say, have never crossed his threshold.

Collecting Edith

GEORGE RAMSDEN

In March 1984, full of the joys of spring and possibly slightly mad, I bought the library of the American novelist Edith Wharton from Maggs Bros., the London booksellers, and subsequently discovered that it was incomplete.

Maggs had purchased about two thousand books from Edith Wharton's godson, Colin Clark, which for forty-seven years had been at Saltwood Castle in Kent. Here his father, the art historian Kenneth Clark, Edith Wharton's friend, had completely integrated them into his own library, which complicated the process of identification and extraction. This had been supervised by Colin's brother Alan who was by then the custodian of Saltwood.

Three uncomfortable years later I was anxious to see if anything had been missed in that initial operation. Tristan Garel-Jones, an MP friend of Alan Clark's at that time, thought I had little chance of getting any books out of him. 'The maverick Mr Clark' didn't need money and his wife hated things to leave Saltwood. However, a visit was arranged.

The castle is completely detached from its suburban neighbourhood and well defended. You arrive at the locked wooden gates of a barbican, locate an entry-intercom and contemplate the painted silhouettes of Rottweilers. Dogs howl when you press the buzzer.

Alan's wife Jane apologized for his having had to go up to London. She took me across a lawn to the Great Hall, once an Archbishop's Hall of Audience and which Kenneth Clark had turned into his library. There is a photograph of him here, his womenfolk in the background, examining a portfolio at the long refectory table; and here, at various junctures in his political career, Alan would kneel to speak to God. The room is a place of deep peace and ancient damp. The bookshelves run high up bare stone walls and are covered in netting to keep birds off.

I had had three years to learn about Edith Wharton and now found many books which bore the unmistakable marks of her ownership. I longed to add them to the library, but how?

At this point Alan's sister Colette decided to sell the bungalow that Kenneth Clark had built for his retirement and which she had inherited. It contained the cream of her father's books. Her brother had tried to persuade her not to sell them, but without success. Fortunately I was able to track some of them down to a shop in London. Kenneth Clark's autobiography and other writings led me to books closely associated with his life, friendships and interests. There were various Bernard Berenson volumes, including one that the young Kenneth Clark had annotated extensively at Winchester, a fine collection of Aubrey Beardsley, Maurice Bowra's books with inscriptions (dull but regular), an unpublished Betjeman poem in manuscript which fell out of one of Edith Wharton's books, Alberti, Van Gogh's Letters, and other art books with his index-notes on the endpapers. Armed with these, my prospects brightened. I offered them in part exchange for Edith Wharton's books.

On my second visit Alan Clark took me to every location in the castle that might harbour Edith's books, including an archive room up a narrow stone staircase. There were no books there but I noticed a landscape by Cézanne, a lithographic reproduction possibly, dusty and folded. Cleaned up, it might have graced the wall of a Fulham kitchen. However, my offer was instantly dismissed. Clark said it wouldn't buy him a plate of shrimps at Wilton's.

He asked me to find various books for him in the trade, Eric Gill's *Twenty-five Nudes* and Dangerfield's *The Strange Death of Liberal England* among them. Of the books I coveted he had an inconvenient fondness for a copy of William Orpen's *An Onlooker in France*,

1917–1919 from which he had once removed Edith Wharton's bookplate. Loose in the book was a postcard with a colour illustration on silk of a town in flames, captioned 'Bapaume, 1917'. On the back a Tommy had written that a rat had got into his tent and eaten his birthday cake. Clark loved everything about this copy, even the stains on the faded green cloth, and was reluctant to exchange it for a better one. I soon got a letter from him – 'I fear I have terrible news. I am pining for the Orpen' – in which he proposed 'a little light subterfuge' whereby we'd stick Wharton's bookplate into another copy. Then he relented, but he clearly had strong feelings about the Great War: he had toured the battlefields of France and Flanders on his honeymoon and been outspoken about the generals in *The Donkeys*, while Edith Wharton had herself visited the Front and lived through the war in the rue de Varenne in Paris, and been decorated for her work on behalf of refugees.

A pattern developed whereby I would identify Edith Wharton books on one visit and negotiate for them on the next, often several months later. I was required to 'replace the divots' with suitable books, normally with the emphasis on appearance rather than content. In Clark's study, for instance, he favoured the mellow tones of old calf, whereas in the Great Hall he'd diversify a uniform run of books with a splash of gilt. As we suited my imported volumes to the shelves, I remarked that it was like flower-arranging. To his credit he entirely agreed – no cant there.

My last visit to Saltwood in Alan Clark's lifetime was in April 1999, only a month or two before he became ill. Up till then I had never been denied any Wharton book but I was still uncertain whether I would obtain them all, for I knew I was trying the Clarks' patience. On a previous occasion Alan had said, 'I find it admirable that you should devote your whole life to reconstructing Edith Wharton's library; it is also a *thundering* nuisance.' Now a sizeable heap of her books was at stake. He rubbed away at the lozenge-shaped panes of an oriel in the Great Hall while I arranged books. A film crew was expected (the windows were probably being cleaned for their benefit). It is a big room so we spoke up clearly. He enquired after my father, his fag-master at school – how old was he? Why wasn't he in the Lords? – questions he often asks of himself in his diaries. What did my elder brother do? I said that he farmed – 'you mean he runs the estate?' – and hunted the hounds, expecting him to mind that. But no, he said he wasn't anti-hunting . . .

Meanwhile I didn't seem to have brought enough books. 'Ah,' said Clark, coming over to inspect my progress, 'you're running out of ammo.' Then, climbing to a high shelf, I dislodged something with my foot and it crashed to the floor. 'You foolish youth!' he cried. We found a framed Christmas card and broken glass. 'The Queen Mum! Jane will be furious. The deal's off . . . a bad omen, anyway.' However, as he put it, 'we finally dealt'. After I had loaded the Wharton books into my Renault Five, we drove the fifty yards to the gateway. 'You haven't swindled me, have you?' he asked, with his feet on the dashboard. I didn't think there had been any swindling. We had had one thing in common, however, the feeling that certain books do belong in certain places. To that extent we were men of principle.

With the kind co-operation of a generation of Clarks (Alan, Colin, Colette) more than six hundred books were reunited with Edith Wharton's library. Jane Clark has come across a few more during the past five years. When I turn up to collect them, Saltwood is still an enchanted oasis, but Alan Clark lies beneath a large stone on the lawn.

In January 2006 Edith Wharton's library returned to the shelves of one of her former homes, The Mount, near Lenox in Massachusetts, which she built and lived in from 1905 to 1913. The Mount and its gardens are open to the public annually from May to October. A version of this article first appeared in *Matrix* (No. 25, December 2005).

The apotheosis of a bookseller: the First Lady, Laura Bush, with George Ramsden at The Mount, 24 April 2006 (© Kevin Sprague)

GEORGE RAMSDEN worked at Heywood Hill's bookshop for three years, but for the last twenty-five he has run Stone Trough Books, first in Camberwell and now at 38 Fossgate in York, trading in secondhand books, editing, book-designing and publishing (see *Slightly Foxed*, No. 5).

Anna and the Bazooka

VIRGINIA IRONSIDE

I can drop Anna Kavan's name among the most literary of my friends and their brows furrow and they confess that, even though thirteen of her books are still in print, and a second biography of her life, *A Stranger on Earth*, by Jeremy Reed, came out this spring, they've never heard of her, let alone read a word by her.

Anna Kavan wasn't her real name. She was born Helen Woods but changed her name to Helen Ferguson. Then, when she married, she became Helen Edmunds, but after her divorce (or was there a divorce? Everything about the woman is so mysterious) she destroyed all her diaries and papers, and invented a new birth date, a new physical appearance and a new literary style. 'I was about to become the world's best-kept secret, one that would never be told. What a thrilling enigma for posterity I should be,' she wrote.

The following books by Anna Kavan are all available from Peter Owen: *A Charmed Circle* (1929) · Hb · 317pp · £15.75 · ISBN 0720609283; *Asylum Piece* (1940) · Pb · 212pp · £9.95 · ISBN 0720611237; *Change the Name* (1941) · Hb · 254pp · £15.50 · ISBN 072060883X; *Sleep Has His House* (1948) · Pb · 190pp · £9.95 · ISBN 0720611296; *Eagle's Nest* (1957) · Hb · 256pp · £13.95 · ISBN 0720628350; *Who Are You?* (1963) · Pb · 117pp · £8.95 · ISBN 0720611504; *Ice* (1969) · Pb · 170pp · £9.95 · ISBN 0720612683; *Mercury* (1994) · Hb · 170pp · £14.95 · ISBN 0720609402; *A Stranger Still* (1995) · Hb · 253pp · £15.95 · ISBN 0720609550; *The Parson* (1995) · Pb · 106pp · £8.50 · ISBN 0720611407.

The following biographies of Anna Kavan are also available from Peter Owen: David Callard, *The Case of Anna Kavan* (1992) · Hb · 168pp · £16.95 · ISBN 0720608678; Jeremy Reed, *A Stranger on Earth* (2006) · Pb · 208pp · £13.99 · ISBN 072061273X.

In fact she turned herself into such an enigma that she's been nearly forgotten, though it's not as if people haven't discovered her. They discover her endlessly. When Jonathan Cape published *Asylum Piece*, her first book written as Anna Kavan in 1940, she wrote: 'At last I did produce something really good, something quite out of the ordinary, if I say it myself. The preliminary reviews were first rate, everything seemed set for success. You've really brought it off this time, Jonathan said. Then the war started. That was the end of that.'

She worked for Cyril Connolly at *Horizon* in the '40s; Anaïs Nin described her as 'an equal to Kafka'; Doris Lessing rediscovered her and so did J. G. Ballard; Brian Aldiss declared her to be a truly great science fiction writer and voted *Ice*, a metaphysical thriller, the Best Science Fiction Novel of 1967; and then, twelve years ago, David Callard wrote the first biography of her, *The Case of Anna Kavan*. But despite being discovered so often, despite being one of the most original English female writers of her generation, Anna Kavan remains, to most people, a puzzle.

One of the problems is that she's no Joanna Trollope. Not for her cosy scenes of domestic harmony and disharmony. No one lives happily ever after in a book by Anna Kavan – and they didn't live happily ever after in the more family-orientated books she wrote under her earlier names, either. She writes of being locked up in mysterious asylums, surrounded by deranged people; she writes of paranoia, of suspicion, of chilling loneliness and imprisonment. Hers is a terrifying inner landscape of death and evil – in which her only friends are animals or birds who come to comfort her. In one of her stories the hero is incarcerated in a cruel prison where the guards play table tennis with rats instead of balls, and in many ways her writing is reminiscent of Kafka, from whom she derived her pseudonym.

Often a short story of hers involves waiting for a reprieve or a punishment that never comes. 'To whom can one appeal when one does not even know where to find the judge? How can one ever hope to find one's innocence when there is no means of knowing of what one has been accused?' she wrote in 'At Night', a story in *Asylum Piece.*

In another two-page story, 'A Certain Experience', Kavan tells of a bitter-sweet experience.

> For instance, it can be stated plainly that I was condemned, that I was imprisoned, that I had given up hope, and that I was then delivered and set free without stipulations. I can describe the courtyard with its high, spiked walls, where shuffling, indistinguishable gangs swept the leaves which the guards always re-scattered to be swept again. I can describe the peep-hole in the hookless door, the hard, unsleeping eye-bulb in its cage. I can describe the smells in the corridors, the sounds ambiguously interpreted, the sights from which eyes were averted hastily. I can describe the hands under which I suffered; I can describe the visitor with the rolled umbrella who announced my release.

But she never is released; and that is one of Kavan's happier tales.

I love her books partly because, having suffered acute depression myself, I know the territory she's talking about. I've never been in asylums like the ones Anna Kavan frequented but, like her, I know the interface between reality and hell. And because she writes of it with such simple honesty and elegance, her books are curiously reassuring to a fellow-sufferer.

Anna Kavan was born in Cannes in 1901 to a mother who was far more interested in socializing than in looking after her strange child. She was dumped on nannies and aunts, and then sent to boarding schools in America and France, and finally to Malvern Girls' College, which she hated. (At school, she later wrote, 'One day when I combed my hair in front of the mirror, my mother looked out at me with her face of an exiled princess. That was the day I knew I was unhappy.')

Her father was a remote figure who jumped overboard to his death from a liner bound for South America, and Anna's mother was left so badly off that even though Anna begged to go to Oxford, she refused, preferring to push her into marriage with one of her own cast-off lovers, Donald Ferguson, an engineer on the Burmese railways. (He apparently beat rats to death with a tennis racquet, and became the model for the ghastly guards in the prison.) Living a wretched life in Mandalay, Anna spent her time writing.

The books she wrote as Helen Ferguson are, on the surface, just humdrum Aga-sagas. Their plots involve strict fathers, love-affairs, unhappy marriages, unrequited love, spinster sisters, but read any one of them and you'll find that they're completely unlike the domestic novels of today. Threading through them are a horror and a cruelty that are menacing and claustrophobic. Clearly they reflect how Anna felt in her wretched marriage in the Far East.

Eventually she fled, leaving behind her young son, and fell in with a group of racing drivers in the South of France. 'I liked them because they were honest,' she wrote. 'Not one of them ever told me life was worth living.' It was these self-destructive men who introduced her to heroin. She was halfway there already, having been recommended cocaine by a tennis coach 'to improve her serve'.

It's not surprising that the next husband she found, the artist Stuart Edmonds, was an alcoholic. By now, her son Bryan had returned to her, and they all lived a chaotic but reasonably happy life in Buckinghamshire. Anna had, during one period of her life, spent time at the Central School of Arts and Crafts and had been taught by the charismatic Ukrainian teacher, Bernard Meninski (a hero of my father, who was also taught by him and who went on to teach alongside him in the '40s – I often wonder whether he ever taught Anna Kavan).

In Buckinghamshire, Anna wrote and painted. But slowly Stuart drank more and more; and no doubt Anna used heroin more and more. Their marriage ended with the first of her three suicide attempts.

She wrote of one attempt in her book *My Soul in China*:

> All at once, despair coils itself neatly inside my head, leaving no room for any other feeling. I snatch a steaming cup of tea from somewhere and with the utmost haste I start dissolving in it tablets of veronal, tuinal, sodium amytal, etc, etc. As if I were catching a train and hadn't a second to lose. I keep stirring more and more tablets into the hot tea, until the contents of the cup are solid like blancmange; this nauseous mess I cram into my mouth with a spoon.

These suicide attempts always resulted in a visit to a clinic – but detoxing never worked for Anna. Before a few days were out, she began using again. 'Heroin has saved my life and kept me from madness,' she wrote. Her gear she called her 'paraphernalia', and her syringe was referred to as her 'bazooka'. Indeed one of her collections of short stories is called *Julia and the Bazooka*, and the first story in it is about a young woman being discharged from a detox clinic – and being terrified once she's faced with the streets of London.

But Anna wasn't the kind of down-and-out addict that we know today. After her marriage to Stuart collapsed, she moved to a fashionable house in Campden Hill and devoted her life to writing, painting, doing up houses – and taking drugs. Though heroin was illegal, it was easily available on the black market. Luckily, during one of her many unsuccessful detoxes, she met a psychiatrist, Dr Karl Theodore Bluth, with whom she had an intense but platonic relationship (he was married). It was then that she abandoned her past identities and turned into Anna Kavan; and it was Dr Bluth who persuaded her to register with the Home Office as a heroin addict – there were only around two hundred registered addicts in 1949 – so that he could supply her legally. He became, in effect, her dealer.

Bluth's death in 1964 caused Anna intense grief but also raised the immediate problem of how to supply her habit. In 1961, an interdepartmental government committee had recommended that heroin addicts should attend out-patient clinics to get their fixes. Terrified that she might be forced to undergo compulsory detoxification, Anna Kavan frantically stockpiled her supplies.

So why do I love this gloomy and hopelessly addicted author, who once wrote that 'I have an unhappy nature and there is something incomprehensible about me which invites misfortune.' Perhaps because she suffered such a terrible sense of alienation and despair. When Anna Kavan writes of a nameless heroine who goes to beg for mercy from mysterious superiors who are punishing her for a crime she cannot name but of which she knows she is, in some way, guilty, I know exactly what she is talking about. 'I am freezing with cold and loneliness down there in the fog,' she says. 'Please be kind to me. Let me share a little bit of your sunshine and warmth. I won't be any trouble to you.'

Anna Kavan died of a heart attack in the winter of 1968, on the very evening she was due to attend a Notting Hill party given by her publisher Peter Owen to introduce her to her greatest admirer, Anaïs Nin. She was found lying on her bed, her head on the Chinese box in which she kept her drugs. Later, the police admitted that they found enough heroin in her house to 'kill the whole street'.

Though her writing is more surreal, Anna Kavan had a lot in common with Jean Rhys. They were both addicts, albeit of different substances, and both were paranoid, damaged, alienated. In many ways, too, she is reminiscent of those self-destructive stars of the screen and stage – Marilyn Monroe, Elvis Presley, Jimi Hendrix, Kurt Cobain, Janis Joplin.

Nevertheless, she continued writing till the end, sending her stories to her publisher pinned together with a hypodermic needle.

VIRGINIA IRONSIDE is best known as an agony aunt with the *Independent*. She has written over fifteen books, and has been instrumental in organizing the gravestone for the writer Julian MacLaren-Ross. Her *No! I Don't Want to Join a Bookclub*, a fictionalized diary about being 60 and a granny, has just been published.

Not so Bad, Really

FRANCES DONNELLY

When I first read Barbara Pym's *Excellent Women* in 1979 it certainly provoked a strong response, but hardly the admiration the cover blurb demanded for 'one of the finest examples of high comedy of the last century'. I felt fury mixed with bafflement.

For me, at that time, every novel was a possible blueprint for how to live your life. Borne along on the second wave of feminism, the only thing I and my friends were sure of was that we didn't want lives like our mothers'. Exactly what we did want wasn't clear. But what I didn't want *in spades* was a life like that of Mildred Lathbury, one of the 'excellent women' of the title.

To my youthful eye the novel was the summation of every bad old thing I'd left home to escape. Mildred is the daughter of a deceased vicar living a small and hopelessly genteel life in London just after the Second World War. Her life is exemplary – and dull. When not listening to talks on the BBC Home Service she rinses her stockings – not nylons, for the only Americans Mildred meets are anthropologists, who are not known for giving a girl a good time. She works for the Distressed Gentlewoman's Association and her local church.

The plot hinges on the marital affairs of a smart young couple who take the flat below, and a designing minx who sets her fur cape at the vicar. Mildred's role is to be made use of by almost every character in the book. A conclusion of sorts is reached when a priggish young man called Everard Bone, who I concluded incredulously

---

Barbara Pym, *Jane and Prudence* (1953) · Pan · Pb · 256pp · £5.99 · ISBN 0330323040; *Excellent Women* (1952) will be reprinted this October by Pan.

must be the romantic hero, asks Mildred to help with – i.e. do for free – the typing, proofing and indexing of his new book. 'I've noticed that *Excellent Women* always seems to make men uncomfortable,' mused Ms Pym somewhat disingenuously. In a sequel, *Jane and Prudence*, Everard and Mildred get married.

I was not so utterly self-absorbed that I didn't notice and appreciate a certain gentle malice informing this even narrative. And I grudgingly admitted that it was quite funny in places. But overall it made me whinny with frustration. Why didn't Mildred stop being so meek? Make herself over? Raise her self-esteem? Take control of her life? Remember, this was 1979, a particularly unfortunate moment to be making a stand for the virtues of restraint, self-effacement and humility. It was the year Mrs Thatcher was elected, the year that *Scruples* by Judith Krantz, the first of the gold-embossed 'entitlement' novels, was published over here. The voice of the self-help guru was being heard in the land. Credulous young women like me were being assured that it was possible to have a high-powered job, an Olympian sex life, gorgeous clothes, lovely homes, contented children and marriage to a very rich man with no visible sign of strain. All you needed was a Filofax and a bit of focus. We were confident that we could 'Have It All', whilst all Barbara Pym could offer was a faint 'Not So Bad, Really'.

Time passed. 'Having It All' turned out to be 'Doing Nothing Properly'. Common sense made a belated reappearance. Many gold-embossed novels found their way to Oxfam. And I discovered how very much I enjoyed revisiting the drab postwar world of Barbara Pym.

For me, one of the most powerful aspects of *Excellent Women* is the extraordinarily vivid picture it draws of London just after the war. Without labouring the point, Pym immerses the reader in a landscape of worn-out people who have won the war but are too exhausted to enjoy the peace. London life is one of sooty, damaged buildings and an atmosphere of privation, cold and rootlessness. The lunchtime services Mildred attends take place in a bomb-damaged church, the side aisles full of smashed cherubs and chipped tablets. Food rationing means that the acquisition of a small joint of meat is an occasion worth celebrating by inviting a friend round to share it; and when the rector paints a wall with an old pot of pre-war cream distemper and is doubtful about the resulting colour, no one present can reassure him that it's authentic, for none of them can remember what cream looks like.

But my renewed interest was not simply a wave of nostalgia for Kardomahs or carrying a fish wrapped in newspaper in a string bag. There were so many things about this story with which I identified. Like Mildred's, my growing up had been shaped by religion. My family's life had also revolved around the local church. For us the seasons were marked by the colour of vestments as well as the colour of leaves, and it was not until I left home that I discovered that social occasions could and did take place without a tea urn. I also recognized and thoroughly enjoyed Barbara Pym's description of bad behaviour at the church jumble sale.

What gave the novel an added piquancy was that, in spite of her obvious religious commitment, Barbara Pym was remarkably clear-eyed and unsentimental about the Church. Her clergy are a group of men acting out their vocations with a distinct lack of conviction. The Church she describes is no longer a vital force in society. On the contrary, it is peopled by uncertain shepherds and a shrinking flock made up almost entirely of 'excellent women'. And 'excellent women' usually means spinsters. Even those lucky enough to get a proposal of typing seem destined to remain childless. In this respect at least we Romans had the Anglicans completely trumped: there were no children in their congregations – so unlike the life in our own dear noisy pews.

What I had failed to see in the Scornful Seventies was the social commentary, the extent to which Mildred is kept in her place by the teachings of both Church and society. Barbara Pym is often compared with Jane Austen, who would certainly have recognized Mildred's world. Like Jane Austen, Mildred lived at a time when women still had to look almost solely to marriage for fulfilment. This was fine if you drew Mr Darcy or Henry Tilney in the marriage lottery, less good when your ticket turned out to entitle you to become Mrs Everard Bone. Yet this title at least gave Mildred status and an identity in a world that could only offer a spinster the role of 'excellent woman', or doormat to all comers.

Because that world is so small and contained and usually middle-class, Barbara Pym's novels are easily dismissed as interesting but marginal. But, as I came to realize, they are full of wit, balance, sly observation and a cheering sense of the ridiculous. My own self-dramatizing search for literary ways to live my life rather dwindled away after I had children. Living became more a matter of crashing on with things, regardless of any blueprint. A day that could be concluded with the thought 'Everyone got fed and no one died' was a good one.

For nostalgic reasons I reread *Scruples* recently and preposterous tosh though it is, I was still affected. No story of a girl shedding a great deal of weight in adolescence will ever lose the power to move me. Heavily plotted novels with facile resolutions have their place – usually on a Friday night when the human spirit is known to be at a very low ebb. But the more lasting messages of how to live your life I found, after all, in *Excellent Women*. Mildred's keen eye for the ridiculous, her integrity, her lack of self-pity and her intense pleasure in small things now seem to me admirable. Coping mechanisms they may be, but there are worse ways of dealing with life.

After twenty-five years as a producer and presenter on Radio 4, FRANCES DONNELLY moved to East Anglia where she is working on her third novel. In addition, maddened by the demise of the Kardomah, the ABC and Joe Lyons, she has set up her own bakery business, Homemade Cakes of Ditchingham, and supplies a number of genteel teashops in Norfolk and Suffolk.

The Quiet Sicilian

JOHN DE FALBE

I first read Giuseppe di Lampedusa's novel *The Leopard* while I was in Palermo in 1981, at the age of 18. It was one of those defining reading experiences which are not always easy to explain but which have to do with a deep sense of recognition. Through the alchemy of fictional characters and the way in which they engage with their world, you are taken somewhere (psychologically, morally, emotionally) that you do not usually expect to go, and the journey reveals to you something about yourself and the world you inhabit. You may also recognize with awe that the author has achieved something of extraordinary value. Who is this person, you wonder then, and what did it feel like to create this phenomenon? One does not necessarily expect an answer to the second part of this question in an author's biography, but if it is there then you may get that fuzzy feeling of awe all over again.

David Gilmour's biography of Giuseppe di Lampedusa, *The Last Leopard*, was published in 1988. It made a great impression on me, and I have recommended and sold it ever since with confidence. But as the years passed I started to wonder if I wasn't misled by inexperience. I was young when I read it, and had not then read many other biographies of writers. How would it measure up now? I knew it was

---

Giuseppe di Lampedusa, *The Leopard* (1958) · Translated by Archibald Colquhoun · Everyman · Hb · 240pp · £10.99 · ISBN 1857150236

David Gilmour, *The Last Leopard: A Life of Giuseppe di Lampedusa* (1988), is now out of print, but Eland Books (tel 0207 833 0762) have come to the rescue and will reissue it next May.

out of print because we had bought up the end of the print run, and Mr Horse's Mouth at Random House told me lately, on enquiry, that however many copies a couple of fancy independent shops might sell over the next few years, it would never find its way back to the shelves of high street shops and therefore – hands were wrung, I swear – a reprint could not reasonably be contemplated. This and the imminent fiftieth anniversary of *The Leopard*'s first publication were just the incentives needed to drive me crossly, protectively, back to both the novel and the biography of its author.

The facts – who Lampedusa was, and what he did – are almost comically simple. Born in Palermo in 1896, he was the only son of an old aristocratic family whose patrimony was already much diminished. Cosseted as a child, he soon developed a passion for literature. As Gilmour remarks with some surprise, it seems never to have occurred to Lampedusa that he might work, but he served briefly as a soldier during the First World War and then as a rather testy Red Cross official in Sicily during the Second. Otherwise he read, sat in cafés, occasionally went to cocktail parties which he detested, travelled to England and France from time to time, and also to Latvia. For though he never had children, he married a Baltic baroness called Licy, who was a distinguished psychoanalyst. Until late in the Great War, Licy preferred to stay at her castle in Latvia rather than with her husband in Sicily where she had to compete for his attentions with his over-fond mother. But afterwards, when his palace had been bombed and hers was taken over by the Soviets, they lived together in genteel decay in a draughty, second-division Palermo palazzo with a leaky gas boiler. For a few years he gave informal lessons in literature to a couple of young friends, and in 1955, after being diagnosed with emphysema, started writing '*pour m'amuser*'. He died in July 1957 and his novel *The Leopard* was published in November the following year. It became the best-selling book in Italian literary history.

The subject of Gilmour's biography spent most of his life on a chair, and if he wasn't reading then he was groaning at the prospect of his own, and his family's, extinction. How on earth can such unpromising material be made into a riveting book? The apparent contradiction is undoubtedly part of the book's anecdotal charm. But it also explains why it is so remarkable, for Gilmour demonstrates that there is in fact no contradiction. Lampedusa's life was intimately connected to his world. He did not do nothing. There is a temptation to see the dramatic shape supplied by the final writing of his masterpiece as somehow artificial, too good to be true: isn't it just sentimental retrospective piety that makes us want to make sense of this layabout's life as a grand preparation? Gilmour shows that it is not. And if Lampedusa had not written *The Leopard*, what then of the life? It is not enough to say that the question is academic because he did write it: we are forced to recognize the value of the life on its own terms, irrespective of the stupendous posthumous validation.

On the last page of the chapter entitled 'A Baltic Marriage', we read of a young man who sat beside Lampedusa at the aristocratic club in Palermo and could 'get nothing from him but monosyllables'. By now, the reader has been treated to a sharp portrait of Lampedusa's background and early life that is reflected in many respects in *The Leopard*, but though Gilmour writes beautifully and displays a keen sense of the absurd, we might be forgiven for thinking that if the subject isn't quite dead yet then he might as well be – were it not for the mysterious phenomenon that we know is to come. Why is Lampedusa different from his contemporaries, whose behaviour he described as 'the tragic jerking of a class which was watching the end of its own land-owning supremacy, that is, of its own reason for existence and its own social continuity'?

An answer begins to surface in the next chapter, 'The Troubles of Don Giuseppe'. The heading refers to the Lampedusas' domestic arrangements – Licy's final departure from Latvia, the destruction of Palazzo Lampedusa, problems with the Red Cross, the death of the prince's mother. But embedded in it is a brief account of his relationship with his Piccolo cousins, in particular Lucio, with whom

Lampedusa had a literary rapport 'so strong and long-lasting that neither of them bothered to look for other intellectual friends'. But if Lampedusa sometimes seems other-worldly, the Piccolos seem positively alien. 'They not only believed in the existence of spirits but could even sense their presence.' 'The manner in which the Piccolos were able to insulate themselves from the horrors of the Second World War', says Gilmour, after listing the menu for lunch on Easter Sunday 1942, 'was remarkable.'

It is intriguing that a man described by the art historian Bernard Berenson as 'bashful, modest, timid, incredibly courteous' should have felt most comfortable in a nest of nutcases. And as Gilmour starts to describe the prince's life with Licy after the war, we see him come into his own: 'once the diffidence had been conquered, he revealed sides to his character which few people would have suspected: pride, original thought, powerful opinions and a bitter, ironic sense of humour'. Licy's nephew describes visiting the Lampedusas and finding that lunch was non-existent because Licy would still be in bed after working until four in the morning, while Lampedusa would be out of the house, returning later in the afternoon with a few pastries, following his own thoughts and routines. Although deeply conscious that he was a creature of his time and the land of his birth, he was always unusual.

The most conspicuous aspect of this was his astonishing learning, which earned him the nickname '*il mostro*' ('the monster') from his Piccolo cousins. But this learning was not the product of formal study, and it was only late in life that Lampedusa found, among young people, some pleasure in sharing it, first in conversations in a café and then, at Licy's suggestion, during informal literature courses at home. He wrote a thousand pages of notes on English literature from Bede to Graham Greene. 'Not only had he read and remembered all the novels of Scott,' writes Gilmour; 'he knew the plays of the lesser Elizabethan playwrights and the poems of the most minor Restoration poets.'

Giuseppe di Lampedusa (*right*) and his cousin Lucio Piccolo, 1926

He was similarly erudite in French literature, and the breadth of his reading in Russian and Spanish (which he read in the original) was also startling. He believed that people could be understood through their literature and their history but also 'that it was important to investigate everything, not just the large trees in isolation but the undergrowth and flowers as well. They were all part of the great body of literature and contributed to each other's growth.'

As to *The Leopard* itself, it seems that what drove him to write it was the spectacle of his cousin Lucio receiving a prize at a literary festival. Lucio had sent his poems out of the blue to the celebrated poet Eugenio Montale, who impulsively invited him to a literary festival at San Pellegrino in Lombardy. Being apprehensive, Lucio asked *il mostro* to accompany him for moral support. There is a hilarious description of the elderly, unknown Sicilian gentleman turning up and saying nothing. But on his return to Palermo, Lampedusa wrote to an old friend in Brazil, 'Being mathematically certain that I was no more foolish [than Lucio], I sat down at my desk and wrote a novel.'

The story of the novel's creation is intensely moving because

Lampedusa evidently sensed his vocation in the process of writing. Knowing he was ill, urgency suddenly infused all his activities. He didn't want to die any more because he had things to do. The preoccupation with his own extinction might once have looked like sluggishness. But he was never mentally sluggish, just solitary and ironic. Despite his illness, he had huge resources of energy to apply to his new project.

Someone recently said to me that he thought there was too much lit. crit. at the end of *The Last Leopard*. Yet the story of *The Leopard*'s critical reception is of great relevance – not least because it contributed to the novel's success. The book had originally been turned down by several publishers. Once published, it quickly became a bestseller despite (or because of) being savaged by many distinguished critics Besides the Catholics who disapproved of Lampedusa's pessimism and the Sicilian apologists who didn't like his portrait of Sicily, there were Marxist historians who attacked what they imagined to be his view of history and influential critics from Italy's intelligentsia who had spent the years since the Second World War advocating their own rigid interpretations of 'commitment', 'progressiveness' and 'experimentation' in literature. Lampedusa's beautiful prose and well-drawn characters did not fit the mould.

We still have our equivalents of these critics today, and Gilmour's shrewd account of *The Leopard*'s reception, and the light it sheds on that novel, are a warning for our own times. It is instructive too to remember, in these days when every book is either trumpeted as a masterpiece or abandoned, that Lampedusa believed that ground-cover literature matters as well as the trees. Whether *The Last Leopard* is a tree (as I think) or just a flower, it should be read by anyone who loves reading.

JOHN DE FALBE has been selling books at John Sandoe's in Chelsea for 20 years. He is the author of two novels, *The Glass Night* and *The Bequest*, and hopes to have another published next year.

Under the Mulberry Tree

JUSTINE HARDY

Kurdish was a term I heard long before I had any real sense of the world, of where Iran, Iraq, Syria and Turkey are, or what cultural and religious intolerance mean. When I was about 7, a Kurdish girl called Hozan showed me how her people danced at weddings and at great moments of celebration, stamping, swirling and clicking her tongue. She was 15, and to me she was glamour personified, spinning in a field, her tiny denim shorts alarmingly far up her bottom, her head thrown back. This was in the mid-Seventies, in Oxfordshire, and Hozan's family was encamped with some local Romany gypsies. At about the same time, in March 1975, the Shah of Iran signed a treaty with Saddam Hussein. The Kurds of Iraq thereby lost all their external support. And so they began to be exterminated.

The Kurds, scattered across much of the Middle East, are the largest population in the region without a homeland of their own, and their recent history is also the story of the changing political maps of the twentieth century. Hiner Saleem's memoir of his childhood in Kurdistan, *My Father's Rifle*, begins:

> My grandfather had a good sense of humour. He used to say he was born a Kurd, in a free country. Then the Ottomans arrived and said to my grandfather, 'You're Ottoman,' so he became an Ottoman. At the fall of the Ottoman Empire, he became

---

Hiner Saleem, *My Father's Rifle: A Childhood in Kurdistan* (2005) · Translated by Catherine Temerson
Atlantic · Pb · 176pp · £9.99 · ISBN 1843543125

> Turkish. The Turks left and he became a Kurd again in the kingdom of Mahmoud, King of the Kurds. Then the British arrived, so my grandfather became a subject of His Gracious Majesty and even learned a few words of English.
>
> The British invented Iraq, so my grandfather became Iraqi, but this new word, Iraq, always remained an enigma to him, and to his dying breath he was never proud of being Iraqi; nor was his son, my father Shero Selim Malay.

The story of Saleem's family is the story of a people who are Muslim but not Arab, whose land has been fought over, whose culture has been trampled.

Saleem himself was born in Iraqi Kurdistan in 1954. His father, Shero, was the radio operator for General Barzani, the leader of the Kurdish patriots. This meant that he was also a freedom fighter, and the tool of his trade was a Brno, the Czech rifle of the title, a weapon long out of date by the time this story begins.

Saleem is now a film-maker based in Paris, and it is with his powerful visual sense that he draws us into the world of his boyhood. Early on in the book he leads us up a stepladder to the roof where his cousin Cheto keeps his stunt pigeons. And there he throws the birds up into the air, to watch them tumble back down out of the blue sky. In this way he draws us through the lushness of his life as a child in full Technicolor close-up. The rawness that follows, the persecution of his family and of his people, is stripped down to bare black and white. His spare use of language leaves the white page beyond the words heavy with the unwritten.

> Seated under the mulberry tree in the garden of our beautiful old house, my mother was seeding pomegranates. I could see only the tip of her flowery scarf. The pulp from the seeds colored her hands and her face was stained with the red juice of the autumn fruit. Me, I was squatting on my heels stuffing myself.

Saleem was 11 and this was how he remembered the scene that began the end of his boyhood. This minute and careful rendering is immediately followed by the arrival of the pro-government militia in search of a cousin, thought to be a sympathizer of General Barzani, the same man for whom Saleem's father had fought. Seven of the men of Saleem's family are shot in the flight that follows the scene under the mulberry tree.

The traditional structure of their life ended that day. They fled, and they went on running from Saddam's men, living in caves up in the mountains as planes flew over, bombing the villages of Kurdish resistance. Saleem's father picked up his old rifle again to join the *peshmergas*, the Kurdish fighters. The word translates as 'he who looks death straight in the face', and they did, again and again. 'But what could he do with a Czech rifle dating from the 1940s?'

The hopelessness of their dream for an independent Kurdistan becomes clear as the politicians on the world stage withdraw their support and Saddam's power increases. So comes the signing of the treaty between the Shah and Saddam in 1975: 'I saw *peshmergas* commit suicide in despair. Others wanted to hide in the mountains and resist, but the general understood that we were caught in an inescapable net: the choice was between accepting defeat or extermination. We took the road to exile.'

Saleem later returned to Iraq with those of his family who had survived, but the time of mulberry and pomegranate trees had gone. Their world was now controlled by the storm troopers and secret police of Sadaam's Ba'ath party.

This was a world of constant fear: fear of being watched or heard, of being handed over to the authorities, imprisoned or shot – levels of fear that young Saleem realizes are becoming the status quo for his family, and his people. And so he decides to escape.

Hiner Saleem ends his book with brief descriptions of what happened to each of the protagonists, both on the smaller stage of his life and the wider one of Iraqi politics. Each one is poignant and the few lines are shadowed with subtext. He closes the book with just three and a half stark lines about liberation after oppression: 'On April 9, 2003, the coalition forces that had entered Iraq on March 19 conquered Baghdad, and Saddam Hussein's regime was toppled.'

As I finished reading, I wondered where Hozan and her family might be, and whether the women were still spinning, arms in the air, heads thrown back, tongues clicking, in a field in another corner of exile.

JUSTINE HARDY's most recent book, *The Wonder House*, is a novel set in Kashmir.

In a Class of His Own

JEREMY LEWIS

Books that make one laugh out loud are far rarer than one likes to think, and the subject of endless and often heated debate. P. G. Wodehouse usually comes out top, but although I loved him in my twenties, I have lost the appetite in late middle age: comicality needs to be combined with sadness, a sense of the absurd with a countervailing melancholy, and Wodehouse's genial socialites seem too lacking in humanity, too short on Chaplinesque pathos, to engage me as much as they once did. One of my candidates for the funniest book ever written – battling it out with Mr Pooter, James Lees-Milne's *Another Self*, and a great deal of Evelyn Waugh – is H. F. Ellis's *The Papers of A. J. Wentworth BA*, a work that is all too redolent of familiar human frailties.

A. J. Wentworth is an old-fashioned prep-school master of the pompous, bustling, self-important variety: utterly ineffectual at controlling his pupils but much given to ferocious rhetoric and the consoling saws of his trade, he has been teaching maths at the school for most of his life, and the end of his career is in sight.

Written, like *The Diary of a Nobody*, in diary form, the book begins on a note of crisis. Enraged beyond endurance by a pestilential boy called Mason, Wentworth has hurled a copy of Hall & Knight at the wretched youth, but misaimed and brought down another pupil instead. 'It has been suggested that it was intended to hit Hopgood II. This is false. I never wake up sleeping boys by

---

H. F. Ellis, *The Papers of A. J. Wentworth BA* (1949)
Prion · Hb · 160pp · £8.99 · ISBN 185375398X

throwing books at them, as hundreds of old Burgrove boys will be able to testify,' he tells us. Unmoved by his teacher's fury, Mason continues to distract and defy with loathsome insouciance. 'I never overlook impertinence, and I gave Mason a talking to which he will, I think, remember as long as he lives,' Wentworth would have us believe after he has failed to quell yet another act of defiance.

Regarded as an incompetent buffoon by pupils and colleagues alike – these include Matron and the Headmaster, the Reverend Gregory Saunders MA – Wentworth blunders from one humiliation to another. A pigeon is concealed in his desk and flutters out when the lid is opened (the boy responsible 'will soon learn, whoever he is, that it is a bad mistake to underrate your enemy'), paper pellets fly about the classroom ('This sort of thing has to be put down with a firm hand or work becomes impossible'), and a case of mass insubordination provokes threats of terrible retribution ('It can be imagined that I was in no mood after this to stand any nonsense from anybody, and IIIa found that they had a very different person to deal with this morning from their usual good-natured master'). He topples into a shoe basket, snagging his gown on the wickerwork, gets tangled up in a fishing-rod, and becomes wedged in a drain while out walking with the boys. A new source of irritation is provided by the arrival of Major Faggot, a Terry-Thomas lookalike with bristling moustache and yellowing teeth who maddens Wentworth by smoking his pipe in the corridor, reading to the boys with his feet on the desk and handing out the pink blotting paper reserved for Common Room use only.

'An old-fashioned prep-school master of the pompous, bustling, self-important variety'

And yet, for all his absurdity, Wentworth is an extraordinarily lovable character: unlike Bertie Wooster, he is recognizably one of us, as endearing, absurd and touching as Mr Pickwick, another disaster-prone bachelor of advancing years. Like Mr Pooter, whom he so closely resembles, he made his first appearance in *Punch*, in November 1938, and was published in book form eleven years later – at about the same time that Nigel Molesworth of St Custard's was starting his own career in *Punch*. Comparisons with *The Diary of a Nobody* were inevitable, and deeply resented by Wentworth's amiable creator: but whereas Pooter was restricted to a single volume, the old schoolmaster resurfaced in *A. J. Wentworth BA (Ret'd)*. Published in 1962, it describes how Wentworth, now living in retirement on the South Coast, suffers at the hands of WI ladies and jocular vicars: it has its moments, but *The Swansong of A. J. Wentworth*, published in 1982, is regarded by those in the know as an altogether inferior work.

Wentworth's creator, H. F. Ellis, was a veteran of both *Punch* and prep-school life. Born in 1907, he was educated at Tonbridge and Magdalen College, Oxford. 'You think you're funny,' his fellow-undergraduate John Betjeman once told him, 'well, you are.' Between school and Oxford he had taught at his old prep school near Liphook, and after leaving Oxford he taught for a term at Marlborough. But he found the work uncongenial, and abandoned teaching for the more hazardous life of a writer. A cheque from *Punch* arrived just as he was about to propose to his future wife, and had an emboldening effect.

Sir Owen Seaman, the editor of *Punch*, encouraged Ellis to become a regular contributor; his successor, E. V. Knox, appointed him assistant editor in 1933, in charge of an editorial staff of four. The Ellis house in Roehampton became a rendezvous for fellow-contributors such as A. P. Herbert, Bernard Partridge, E. H. Shepherd and A. A. Milne; congenial ingredients of *Punch* life included long lunches at the Garrick and country-house weekends with a cricket match thrown in. After spending the war in the Royal Artillery, Ellis returned to *Punch* under the editorship of Bernard Hollowood and Malcolm Muggeridge, serving spells as literary and deputy editor. But he took an instant dislike to the next editor, William Davis, and severed all connections with the magazine in 1968. Salvation, however, was at hand in the form of S. J. Perelman, who urged him to become a regular contributor to the *New Yorker*.

Ellis had been an enthusiastic rugger and cricket player at Oxford, and whereas *The Papers of A. J. Wentworth* has remained only fitfully in print, surging on to the bookshelves when an enthusiastic publisher takes up the cause before sinking back into oblivion, Ellis's account of the rules of rugger, *Why the Whistle Went*, has been endlessly reprinted and translated into innumerable languages, including Japanese. He also edited the *Royal Artillery Commemoration Handbook* and co-edited *The Manual of Rugby Football*.

I only met Ellis once, not long before his death in 2000, when I went to interview him for the *Oldie*. He and his wife lived in a remote corner of the Quantocks, and they very kindly invited us to lunch. We soon got lost in a maze of tiny lanes, and arrived at least forty minutes late, gasping and panic-stricken. As we screeched into the drive of a pleasant red-brick house, a tall, distinguished-looking man with aquiline features came out of the front door to greet us. I knew from the back of my Penguin *Wentworth* that Ellis was a chubby-looking cove with moonlike features and a quiff of white hair. 'That's not him,' I told my wife. 'We've obviously come to the wrong house.' She let off the brake, and was just about to rev off down more country lanes when the Duke of Wellington lookalike tapped on the window, introduced himself as H. F. Ellis, and invited us in for a large and restorative gin-and-tonic. Penguin, he told me a few minutes later, had muddled his photograph with that of some eminent child psychologist, albeit of the moon-faced variety. It seemed a very Wentworth-like state of affairs.

JEREMY LEWIS's *Penguin Special: The Life and Times of Allen Lane* has just been reprinted in paperback. He is currently researching a biography of the Greene family, and writing Volume Three of his autobiography.

By the Light of the Ptarmigan

LUCY LETHBRIDGE

When I was a teenager, prowling voraciously round my parents' bookshelves looking for something to read, I found a row of old books that hadn't been looked at for at least fifty years. They were all by Sabine Baring-Gould, polymath, squarson, folksong collector, novelist and possessor of an infectiously insatiable curiosity about pretty well everything from esoteric customs to ways in which to save fuel. Among those dusty Baring-Goulds were novels such as *The Broom Squire* and *Mehalah*, his *Reminiscences* of a ninety-year life, *The Book of Werewolves*, several collections of sermons, *English Folk Songs* (compiled with Cecil Sharp), *Curious Myths of the Middle Ages* and lots of travel books including *Cliff Castles and Cave Dwellings in Europe*, guides to the Riviera and the Languedoc, and *Yorkshire Oddities and Strange Events*. Best of all was *Iceland, Its Scenes and Sagas*

Baring-Gould spent two months in Iceland in 1862. He was 28, not yet ordained, and teaching in a boys' public school, Hurstpierpoint. He had developed a passionate interest in the Norse sagas – a craze that had just begun to grip his contemporaries, though it was nine years before William Morris undertook the same journey and made Norse mythology fashionable. In the sagas Baring-Gould thought he had found an untainted oral storytelling tradition that stemmed directly from a peasant people – a direct link with an ancient and magical past for an industrial world from which the magical was disappearing fast. Many in the nineteenth century,

---

Sabine Baring-Gould, *Iceland, Its Scenes and Sagas* (1863)
Signal Books · Pb · 352pp · £12.99 · ISBN 1902669894

watching the smokestacks of the new age, thought they could see it disappearing before their very eyes: a parson gloomily reflected on the first railways, 'It will be the end of stories.'

Baring-Gould embarked on his tour with characteristic energy, teaching himself along the way to read Old Norse and to speak some Icelandic. He took several notebooks in which to jot down observations, meticulous descriptions of nature, and his own (lengthy) translations of the famous sagas of the Icelandic hero Grettir (years later he wrote a historical novel, *Grettir the Outlaw*). The modern reader might do best to skip the sagas, in which Baring-Gould's prose is at its most purple, with much use of the word 'quoth'. But his descriptions of the extraordinary, eerie topography of Iceland are marvellous. He conjures up a landscape that resembles a vast canvas by John Martin: glaciers, geysers, inky black seas and bottomless icy lakes; a massive, awe-inspiring region, sometimes heavenly, sometimes infernal, where humans are as insignificant as gnats. Here he is in the strange isolated region of the Jökulls:

> The scene of desolation is quite indescribable: a vast trench between walls of rock and heaps of snow; the crags of great height and flat-topped, with bare precipices of green ice and snow resting on them, ready to topple over in avalanches with the least disturbing cause, and bury us under their ruins; here and there a cone of snow which has thus shot to the bottom and has not yet begun to melt; now a smooth sweep of undinted whiteness, rising to the Jökull top, or barred with black steps of rock glazed with frozen streams. Not a bird, nor insect, not a sound.

With these grand natural mysteries as their backdrop, it is little wonder the Icelanders had a rich mythology of ghosts, vampires and mermaids; Baring-Gould was in his element. He saw no inconsistency whatsoever in being a staunch High Anglican and a believer in fairies: it was a source of regret to him all his life that he never met a

Iceland: 'a landscape that resembles a vast canvas by John Martin'

fairy himself. In *Iceland*, he includes a detailed account of the Icelandic counterpart of the Loch Ness Monster – a vast basking eel over fifty feet long called the Skrimsl. He was delighted to hear from locals that it had been sighted the day before he arrived. Baring-Gould had many engaging features and his earnest credulity was the most engaging of all.

He was as interested in ordinary domestic life as in supernatural splendours, and carefully noted down everything he ate on his trip – generally Icelandic moss stewed in milk or stringy whimbrel stew. The Icelanders as a race fascinated him though his interest was always in types rather than individuals, preferring people to conform to the national characteristics with which he endowed them, but he eschewed the gushy romanticism of many contemporary accounts of the rural poor. Baring-Gould may be credulous but he is never sentimental. He dismissed the popular image of Icelanders sitting round blazing fires playing rustic harps and telling sagas, and briskly reported that most of them lived in houses without a fire, and kept warm by piling on stinking sealskins over layers of protective grime. The stench of whale fat and old fish inside their houses was overpowering. The oily ptarmigan made a handy lamp when hung up with a wick threaded through its innards. On the advice of a travellers' handbook he took with him pewter rings decorated with artificial diamonds to use as barter with the natives but he was embarrassed to find that they took them to be an offer of marriage.

There were several other English tourists plodding across Iceland's blowy wastes in the mid-nineteenth century. Baring-Gould related a bizarre encounter with 'a man in shabby garments rather lame' who spoke English and had been travelling in the country for a year. This was Ralph Milbanke, grandson of Byron and later Earl of Lovelace, who had dislocated his thigh on a remote lava-field; he had been nursed back to health by a pastor's daughter with whom he'd fallen in love but who had thrown him over for a local ostler. When the two men met in the bleak tundra of Grimstunga, Milbanke was on his way home to England broken-hearted.

But one of the most enjoyable aspects of *Iceland, Its Scenes and Sagas* is that it reveals a rare and unexpected comic strain in Baring-Gould. It is true that the humour creaks rather than sparkles, but in his travelling companion Mr Briggs ('my portly friend') he unwittingly created a perfect foil for his own patrician intensity. Poor Mr Briggs, athirst for pre-industrial authenticity, is disappointed to find signs of modernity in Iceland, and complains:

> 'There is not the slightest use in coming to Iceland!'
>
> 'How so?'
>
> 'Why it is just like everywhere else! I have been looking in at one of the stores, and what do you think I saw? Crinolines, real crinolines, man! Crinolines! Is it not horrible? We are not beyond the range of fashion yet!'

On another occasion, Mr Briggs sees an Icelandic maiden, a model of the authentic peasant, approaching: 'A houri! A tinted

Venus! A Valkyri!' Baring-Gould, ready with his notebook, slyly noted Briggs's horror when she pulled out a dried stockfish and gnawed vigorously on its bones.

I was asked recently to write on Sabine Baring-Gould, among others, for a forthcoming exhibition on English eccentrics to be put on at the National Portrait Gallery. Baring-Gould would have been surprised, even slightly irritated, to have found himself classed as an eccentric, despite his interest in the peculiarities of other people. He appears rarely to have given a thought to how others saw him. His chief concern is to show us what he sees. *Iceland, Its Scenes and Sagas* may not be the most elegant or the most accurate of travel books, but it is an irresistible testament to boundless enthusiasm.

LUCY LETHBRIDGE is writing a book on twentieth-century servants, to be published by Bloomsbury. She is distantly related to Sabine Baring-Gould.

Prussian Blues

JOHN JOLLIFFE

Of the many missed opportunities of my schooldays, failure to learn German is the one I have regretted most and longest. But in 1949, when the chance arose, German was not the flavour of the month. There was still a large gap in one corner of School Yard where a German bomb had missed a large dormitory of sleeping boys by a few feet. And only a few years earlier, my housemaster had fought with distinction in the Green Jackets, and then married the widow of another officer, killed in battle. He bullied us into opting for elementary science (which has never been the slightest use to me) rather than German for School Certificate.

So I never learned German; and I was never drawn to German literature in translation. But recently, by great good luck, I have stumbled on the novels of Theodor Fontane. Born in 1819 in Brandenburg into a family of Huguenot émigrés on both sides, at the age of 30 he abandoned a career as a pharmacist and set up as a freelance journalist and travel writer. He was thus uniquely well placed to see both sides of the love-hate relationship between Prussia and France, which contained, understandably, a great deal less love on the French side than on the Prussian. He spent four years in England (1855–9), visited Scotland and followed the Tweed in the footsteps of Sir Walter Scott. In 1864 he served as a war correspondent in Schleswig-Holstein, and again in 1870 in the Franco-Prussian War when he was captured and interned for three months. His first, and

---

Unfortunately the Oxford World Classics paperback edition of *Before the Storm* (1878) is no longer in print but copies can be obtained second-hand.

in my opinion greatest novel, *Before the Storm*, was not published until 1878, but it was followed by fifteen others, the best-known being *Effi Briest*, which has been filmed four times, and my second favourite, *Beyond Recall*.

But *Before the Storm* is quite enough to be getting on with. The entire action takes place in the six weeks beginning on Christmas Eve 1812, yet the novel covers 680 pages in the wholly admirable Oxford World Classics paperback edition, which contains an invaluable historical introduction and copious notes that put the story into sharp focus. The context is the retreat through Poland and Prussia of what was left of Napoleon's Grande Armée from the charred ruins of Moscow. (Sadly Fontane was unaware of my favourite story of the time, of Napoleon riding up to a group of muzhiks and asking them imperiously if they had met any French deserters. 'No, Your Majesty,' came the answer, 'you are the first one we have seen.')

One important element in the background of this great novel is the fact that in the days of what is called the Enlightenment, Frederick the Great was a fervent admirer and patron of French tastes, habits and philosophy, and traces of this fashion survived, even after the disaster of Jena, among cultivated, high-ranking ladies of a certain age, further complicating the prevailing mood. But Prussia had been severely humiliated. The Emperor of the French had smashed her army at Jena in 1806, and matters were made worse when he forced her to produce 20,000 troops for his Russian campaign. In consequence, no less than 300 officers resigned from the Prussian army, including Clausewitz. Later, Field Marshal York von Hardenburg withdrew the 20,000 from the war and signed an agreement of neutrality with the Russians. Prussia actually declared war on France in March 1813, and the action of this novel takes place only a few weeks earlier, when the burning political question of the day was whether to attack the French or not.

In one sense *Before the Storm* is a Prussian counterpart to *War and Peace*; but it is constructed with a sense of order of which Tolstoy knew nothing and cared less. Fontane never attempts the extraordinary range of thoughts and emotions which Tolstoy pours out from Prince Andrei when he is wounded at Austerlitz. But if you want to know what happened at Borodino, when and why, Fontane will tell you. In a nutshell, the French, under Murat, Ney and Davoust, found themselves compelled to attack a large Russian army under Kutuzov across the deep bed of a dried-up river, almost a gorge. In the bitter fighting, the French lost a third of their numbers, and the Russians half of theirs. But as usual the Russians could afford their losses far more easily, and Kutuzov's retreat drew the French on to ultimate disaster.

Much of *Before the Storm* consists of dialogue, conducted with a serious but never tedious thoughtfulness, and a humour which enlivens the characters taking part. The story revolves around the family of Vitzevitz, owners of an ancestral estate near Frankfurt-on-Oder, and the von Ladalinskis, survivors from the Partition of Poland, now established in the government hierarchy in Berlin. A double Montague-Capulet situation emerges between the sons and daughters of the respective families, and through their conversations the main characters become real people, so that in varying degrees we can like and respect them, and sympathize with all their problems. Their joys and sorrows, their doubts and certainties throw a convincing light on the sufferings of the human heart, the ups and downs of emotional life, and the changes of mood to which even the steadiest characters are prone.

The cast is beautifully constructed. The chief heroine is the enchanting Renate von Vitzevitz, ultra-loyal to her family and friends, coolly objective in her judgement of issues, slowly advancing into a slightly melancholy but nevertheless satisfying life of inner piety and service, noble but never cloying, never too good to be true. At the opposite extreme is the extraordinary retired General von Bamme, by no means a noble character, full of whims and vanities, assertive and quarrelsome, but fearless and above all honest – a sort of Prussian version of Evelyn Waugh's Brigadier Ritchie-Hook. He too is completely convincing.

And besides the barons and generals and blue-stocking ladies there is the unforgettable figure of Hoppenmarieke, a dwarfish, gypsy-like postwoman, who doubles as a fortune-teller and a local distributor of eggs and also every scrap of local gossip. Unlike the others, she lives in a mud hut with a single door and window, which is neither inside nor outside the domain of the Vitzevitzes. Operating on both sides of the law, and of the village boundary, she is warmly tolerated by the lord of the manor, and as in a fairy story . . . but it would be a pity to reveal the end.

In Fontane's world, authority could be exerted because respect was earned. Values and traditions were shared in a way which has mostly been obliterated by the hideous storms of the twentieth century. With no trace of pomposity, self-importance or condescension, Fontane's characters display (among other things) integrity and dignity, qualities not aspired to, or perhaps even heard of, by the governing classes of Europe today. That is one of the characteristics, though there are several others, which make this book so refreshing, and the characters, and the carefully created atmosphere, so attractive in such an unfamiliar way.

JOHN JOLLIFFE has edited various biographical collections, including *Raymond Asquith: Life and Letters*, and written a history of Glyndebourne. He also reviews regularly for *The Spectator* and *Country Life*.

Shock Waves

JULIA KEAY

Anyone who has ever visited another country and found the food unidentifiable, the language incomprehensible and the rules of behaviour bizarre has experienced some degree of culture shock. Sometimes it's exciting, often it's disconcerting, and if you get ill or lost or inadvertently cause offence it can be frightening. Anne Fadiman's book *The Spirit Catches You and You Fall Down* is about culture shock of a different order altogether. It is the story of what can happen when, even with the best of intentions on both sides, two cultures collide.

The focus of the book is Lia Lee, the daughter of a Hmong refugee couple who settled in California in the 1980s. Originally from central China, the Hmong are a proud, tough, self-reliant people who, according to Fadiman, have only ever wanted to be left alone, 'perhaps the most difficult request any minority can make of a majority culture'. Over several centuries relentless persecution forced the Hmong to retreat from the Yellow and Yangtze river valleys into the highlands of southern China from where, in the nineteenth century, about half a million fled over the border into French Indo-China. Some settled in Thailand and Vietnam; most ended up in the mountains of what is now Laos.

Here, for two or three generations, the Hmong found sanctuary. They built timber houses in the forests; they ate only what they could grow, produce or catch; they treated themselves with herbs when they

---

Anne Fadiman, *The Spirit Catches You and You Fall Down* (1998)
Farrar, Straus and Giroux · Pb · 288pp · £7.99 · ISBN 0374525641

got sick and performed elaborate rituals to placate the spirits which had caused the illness. They had no formal education and little or no contact with the outside world – until the Vietnam War.

Many of their remote mountain villages lay on what came to be known as the Ho Chi Minh Trail, along which the Communists moved arms and supplies from the north to the south of Vietnam via Laos. Since the Americans had promised to respect the neutrality of Laos, they could not deploy their own ground troops in the area. And since the whole ideology of communism was anathema to the independent-minded Hmong, they were easily persuaded to fight for what the Americans promised them would be 'freedom'. Of the estimated 250,000 Hmong living in Laos before the war, as many as 75,000 are thought to have died as a result of the war. Some died fighting; many were killed by the bombs that fell on their villages or by landmines; more still died of hunger and disease when they fled. And when the war was over and the Americans withdrew, leaving Laos in the hands of a Communist government, the Lao People's Party declared the Hmong 'enemies of the state' for having fought on the wrong side.

The Americans airlifted about 3,000 Hmong to safety and, for a while, arranged food-drops for those who remained. But when the relief flights stopped, the Hmong were left to survive by their wits, to die, or to flee the country. Most fled, heading for the safety of Thailand, travelling on foot and by night, carrying their children on their backs, muffling their babies for fear their crying would attract attention; some were caught and shot, and many of the very young and very old died from disease, starvation and exhaustion along the way. Those who made it to Thailand then often spent years in refugee camps before being allowed to emigrate, a few at a time, to the United States.

The Lee family arrived in America from Thailand in 1980. They might as well have arrived on the moon. They spoke no English. They didn't know about electricity. 'They had never seen a toilet before and thought the water in it was to drink or cook with, then when told what it was they didn't know whether to sit or to stand on it. They didn't know that the cans and packets in the grocery store had food in them.' Other newly arrived Hmong refugees 'cooked with motor oil and furniture polish, ate cat food, covered the floors of their apartments with soil and planted vegetables in it and hunted pigeons with crossbows in the streets'.

As culture shock goes, this was severe enough. But at the age of three months Lia Lee started to have seizures. Her parents, Nao Kao and Foua, held traditional Hmong views about the causes and cures of illness and had serious doubts about the efficacy of Western medicine. But before arriving in America they had spent two years in a refugee camp in Thailand, where three of their older children had become very sick. Their only son had died but, after being treated by Western doctors, their two daughters had recovered. So eventually and reluctantly, when Lia's seizures became more frequent and more severe, they took her to hospital where she was diagnosed with epilepsy.

The Hmong know about epilepsy. They call it *quag dab peg*, which literally translates as 'the spirit catches you and you fall down'; the spirit in this case being a soul-stealing *dab*. The Lees concluded that during Lia's soul-installing ceremony, performed when she was three days old, her soul had not been sufficiently firmly attached to her body. A loud noise must have frightened her soul, which had fled in terror and had been stolen by a *dab*. The cure, they told the doctors (through an interpreter), was to bring in a shaman to placate the *dab* in a succession of elaborate ceremonies that would restore Lia's soul.

Highly trained professionals dedicated to relieving suffering and saving lives, the doctors knew nothing of Hmong tradition, but they did know that Lia's epilepsy was treatable with medication. And since Nao Kao and Foua loved their children dearly – the afflicted Lia perhaps most of all – they agreed to let the doctors treat her. The collision was under way. Even with interpreters the Lees couldn't understand what the doctors were telling them. They didn't know what Lia's pills were for, how many they should give her and when; they couldn't read the labels on the bottles; they couldn't take her temperature or fill in her charts; they couldn't understand why if one pill was good, two pills weren't better and three not better still; when Lia showed no sign of improvement they stopped giving her pills at all, treating her instead with herbs grown in an oil drum on a parking lot and seeking advice from a shaman.

Because the Hmong answer to any question is whatever they think the questioner wants to hear (in other words, mostly 'yes'), the doctors didn't realize that the Lees had no idea what they were doing and couldn't understand why Lia's condition wasn't improving. Having changed her medication several times – each time leaving the Lees more confused – they eventually decided that it must be because the Lees were being careless or deliberately obstructive. The doctors got angry; the Lees got scared; and Lia got worse. Eventually her seizures became so severe that the doctors called in the social services; Nao Kao and Foua were accused of child-abuse and – the cruellest of punishments for the family-centric Hmong – Lia was taken away from them and put into care. After a year, when her condition had stabilized under a steadier medical regime, she was allowed home. And the whole agonizing cycle started all over again.

This is a mesmerizing and deeply disturbing story of love, pain, dedication and, ultimately, of almost unbearable irony. Somehow Anne Fadiman (a writer and literary editor rather than an anthropologist) manages to tell it without passing judgement on any of the parties involved. *The Spirit Catches You* should be required reading not only for doctors but for everyone, traveller or stay-at-home, who might ever encounter a culture different from their own.

JULIA KEAY is also a writer and editor; her *Alexander the Corrector* was published in paperback in 2005 and together with her husband John she has just completed a revision of Macmillan's *London Encyclopaedia* for a third edition.

History Man

CHARLES ELLIOTT

It wouldn't do to make excessive claims for Kenneth Roberts. Sixty years ago I might have; he was certainly my favourite writer then, to the extent that when I finally ran out of his books, at the age of 14, in desperation I tried novels by some other Robertses from the same shelf in the Ypsilanti Public Library. They proved to be highly unsatisfactory, nothing at all like Kenneth. What *he* wrote was history, American history, and I was fascinated by history. There seemed to be so little of it around in Michigan.

Approaching Roberts again after a gap of six decades therefore calls for caution. None of us can be completely objective about our childhood fixations, and besides, this man was a best-selling commercial novelist in an age when historical fiction like *Anthony Adverse* and *Gone with the Wind* topped all the lists. (In 1947, for example, no fewer than half the best-selling American books were historical novels, and one of Roberts's – *Lydia Bailey* – was in fourth place. It sold a phenomenal 1,405,936 copies, in hardcover.) In the interests of self-criticism, it seems worth asking: just how good was he?

I've just reread a couple of Roberts's books, starting with his first, the one I remember best – *Arundel* (1930). The title refers to the small Maine seaside town now known as Kennebunkport, but it is basically the story of the terrible overland march in 1775 undertaken by an army under the command of Revolutionary hero – later traitor – Benedict Arnold all the way from the Maine coast to Quebec. The

---

Many of Kenneth Roberts's novels are available in paperback from Down East Books, including *Arundel* (1930) · 496pp · US$18.95 · ISBN 0892723645.

idea, a brave if slightly crackpot one, was a surprise attack on the British garrison there. In the event, the attack was a disaster, though possibly not so great a disaster as the journey itself, a hideous trial of starvation, cold, hostile Indians and a brutally unforgiving wilderness.

Roberts's nominal hero is a lad from Arundel named Steven Nason who, as a member of the expedition, tells the tale. But the real hero of the book is Arnold himself, whose struggle to drive his ill-assorted forces more than 300 miles through some of the worst country in North America, meanwhile contending with everything from wet gunpowder to political squabbles, remains a classic of leadership and endurance to rival Xenophon or Hannibal crossing the Alps. Roberts clearly admires Arnold, yet at the same time conveys a sense of the flaw in his character that would lead him to betray his country five years later.

It may be no accident that in terms of writing – crisp, vivid, sometimes painfully so – the best parts of *Northwest Passage* (1937), Roberts's first major commercial success, also involve a sort of anabasis. This time it is the struggle of a troop of Rogers's Rangers, a famous band of irregulars raised and commanded by another larger-than-life character called Robert Rogers, to get back from a long-distance raid on an Indian village in Canada in 1759. Rogers, a hulking New Englander reputedly more skilled as a woodsman and Indian-fighter than anyone of his time ('He's the size of moose,' says one admiring follower, 'but he goes drifting through the woods like an owl'), is obviously a powerful and brilliantly effective leader, a man after Roberts's heart. Yet as the story goes on following the return from the raid, it gradually becomes plain that for all his strength and energy Rogers will never achieve his grand dreams – to build a personal kingdom on the frontier, to find the Northwest Passage to the Pacific. Instead, he becomes a drunk and a mercenary, and at the end is just another lost soul, probably a traitor, wandering through the chaos of the American Revolution.

For the modern reader, Kenneth Roberts presents certain problems. After My Lai, it will take a strong stomach to accept unquestioningly his enthusiastic account of the Rangers' destruction of an Indian village; his characterization (other than of, say, Rogers and Arnold) tends to be thin; and he can slip into sentimentality. His attitude toward women skirts misogyny. But his grasp of historical detail is stunning and it is hard to fault his prose when he is describing, for example, what it's like to be lost waist-deep in a swamp in a three-day rain turning to snow. Once he gets into his stride, in fact, the pace of his stories is imperative.

Roberts produced in all half a dozen novels, which made him by all accounts comfortably prosperous. He built himself a house on the shore near Kennebunkport and while churning out books seems to have become progressively more crotchety and cantankerous. Not that he was ever one for received opinions – he managed to upset a lot of patriotic American readers by defending the actions of Loyalists during the Revolution, particularly in *Oliver Wiswell* (1940).

But his reputation as 'the irascible Mr Roberts' appears to have been well deserved, given as he was to attacks on professional historians and on anyone else – especially reviewers – who were less than friendly to his books (and many were). It did not help that late in life he took up, of all things, water divining. In the 1930s, when he was building his house, he met a retired game warden-turned-dowser named Henry Gross and became a believer, which for a man of Roberts's nature meant outspoken proselytizer. Gross's feats were indeed amazing – on one occasion he managed to locate water in Bermuda without ever leaving Maine, by dowsing with his forked stick over a map of the island. The two men set up a company together, and Roberts devoted most of the rest of his life to three books on dowsing, all more or less derided.

I once had a chance to meet Kenneth Roberts. Fascinated as I had been by *Arundel* (pronounced, incidentally, 'a-RUN-del' and not, as in Sussex, 'AR-un-del') I got a summer job in Kennebunkport and bicycled from Michigan to the coast of Maine, where I spent a lot of my off-hours in the village library. The librarian knew Roberts and offered to introduce me. I was far too shy. He must have been in his irascible seventies then and thoroughly involved with his forked sticks, so my reluctance may have been just as well.

CHARLES ELLIOTT has been a magazine editor and senior editor of Alfred A. Knopf. He is the author of several books of essays dealing mainly with gardening and garden history, one of which received unaccountable praise in *Slightly Foxed*, No. 2. Although he has lived in Britain for twenty years, he is still an American.

Driven Dotty by Dewey

FRANCES WOOD

In the olden days, when people went to public libraries to borrow books to read, they were probably unaware of the workings of the librarian's mind. Librarians cherish the illusion that the Dewey Decimal Classification system is second nature to readers as well as librarians. Thus the reader in search of books on cookery will head immediately for the 641s, and anyone planning to travel to Germany to look at its architecture can be found in front of the 720s searching specifically for the numbers after the decimal point – 943 – because, as any fool knows, 720 is Architecture and 943 is Germany (although if you were to turn it round, 943. 7 is Czechoslovakia).

Everything has a potential number created from ten main classes, subdivided into ten divisions, each of which has ten sections, and then there is a decimal point, after which the numbers seem to go on for ever. No. 551 is earth sciences. No. 551.5 is meteorology. No. 551. 5784 is snow. No. 551.578409 is 'snow – historical and persons treatment'. So, if you didn't know it was Danish fiction and therefore 839.82, possibly followed by 74 for post-1945, you might classify *Miss Smilla's Feeling for Snow* as 551.578409.

No. 266.02373051 is given as foreign missions of the US in China and is made up of 266.023, 'Foreign Missions', 73 for the United States (though only after the decimal point) and 51 for China, but I'm afraid I don't know where the zeros came from as I'm copying from the Manual. You have to be careful about zeros, however. Rule 5.13 suggests that zeros in the fourth position should be avoided, but they are clearly acceptable elsewhere. I am just going to lie down with a towel (643.52) on my head.

My own memory of using the local library is that, despite an intense and very distressing immersion in the Dewey system, I always looked up at the large boards that read 'History' or 'Travel' or 'Fiction A-F' and then searched below. But Dewey continues to dominate the lives of librarians, and recently all the reference books in the British Library have been 'Deweyed' (not by me, thank heavens), which has made them much harder for me to find.

Melville Louis Kossuth Dewey, who, as one biographer explained, 'successively dropped first the "Louis", then the "Kossuth", then the "le" of "Melville" – and finally, for a while, tried to shorten the "Dewey" to "Dui" ', was born in 1851. He first contemplated life as a foreign missionary, then as a maths teacher until, one day when he was in church, he had a sudden vision of perfect order in every library: 'the solution flasht over me so that I jumpt in my seat and came very near shouting "Eureka!" It was to get absolute simplicity by using the simplest known symbols, the Arabic numerals as decimals with the ordinary significance of nought, to number a classification of all human knowledge in print.'

When you get down to trying to create a Dewey number for a book, the instructions are no more penetrable than the inspiration. The preface to the fourth edition of 1891 contains hints: 'While Italian is always 5, 5 is by no means always Italian. Grammar is 5, Periodicals are 5, Asia is 5, Oratory is 5, etc. Even were it possible, to limit 5 to Italian would waste numbering material and would not justify cost.' On reading this I am immediately seized with the desire to try and create a number for a periodical published in Japanese on the subject of Italian grammar which would involve a lot of 5s, but where would I put the decimal point? Dewey, however, presses on: 'Italian (5), poetry (1) is as plainly 851 with no danger of being mistaken for "poetry of grammar" or "theory of Asia" because the numbers also have that meaning.'

I have never been any good at maths, my distinguished (and expensive) school refusing to put me in for O-level Maths as 'it was not worth the money', so I find anything that involves numbers and decimal points very frightening. In the early 1970s, it was decided that all the books in the Library of the School of Oriental and African Studies, where I was working in the Chinese section, should be assigned Dewey Decimal Numbers. We were handed a reasonably up-to-date copy of the Index and left to get on with it. I found it extraordinarily difficult and spent a lot of time counting on my fingers, rubbing out over and over again, and bursting into tears. Even now, looking along the shelves of the Chinese section, I can still see some terrible long strings of figures that I recognize as my desperate efforts to add, subtract and, on occasions I fear, multiply myself towards a number that summed up the contents of a book.

A major problem was that the Dewey system was essentially all about America, with individual numbers for Free-will Baptists, the Pilgrim Fathers, the Prohibition Party, Herkimer County, NY, and Greenbacks. It wasn't strong on Europe and as for China, well. Dewey divided over two millennia of Chinese history into just three chunks. That left me facing thousands of books on Chinese history to sort logically. Perhaps it is no wonder that I was forced into multiplication and long division as I struggled with the decimal point; and I still remember the day I discovered there was no number for 'Eunuchs', who played a considerable role in Chinese history for over 2,000 years (though there was a special number for 'Elastic-sided boots'). I have frequently raised this point against Dewey and all I can find in the 'Relative Index' to the 20th edition (1989) is 'castrato voices', which doesn't help at all because Chinese eunuchs had notoriously unpleasant voices.

As well as his obsession with creating perfect order in libraries, Dewey was also passionate about saving time by streamlining spelling. This explains why he kept dropping bits off his name. It also explains why I have had such difficulty reading his childhood reminiscences. Writing of a visit with his mother to his uncle's house, he recalled:

> Whyle she was bizi sewing, I slipt into the back yard . . . wher a big dog was gnawing a bone. Probabli I tryd to take it away from him. At all events he tho't me a more tender morsel and proceeded to chew me up . . . Meantym mother, who never feard anything, had mist her babi, lookt out the windo and regardless of the ugli dog, rescued me from his jaws . . .

Apart from the rather sick-making effect of the spelling, the effort is as full of inconsistencies as his Decimal System. He could have removed one of the 'e's from 'proceeded' and tried harder with 'meantym' (meentym?), and I cannot think what induced him to leave the unvoiced 'g' in 'gnawing'.

Though he worked as Director of the New York State Library, Dewey also established a resort on Lake Placid in Essex County, NY, as a sanctuary for sufferers from hay-fever, which afflicted both Dewey and his wife. However, he was forced to resign from 'active leadership in the library profession' in 1905 because of a sentence in the Lake Placid resort handbook which reassured visitors that 'no Jews or strangers or consumptives or other people who can be fairly annoying to cultivated people are received under any circumstances'. Added to this, he was a serial sexual harasser, 'accused of sexual misconduct on the American Library Association Alaska excursion of 1905', and again in 1920 and 1930. This last time, the year before he died, when he was 80 for goodness' sake, he was accused of 'overly familiar behavior with younger women' and had to settle out of court to the tune of $2,145.66. I was quite relieved to discover all this because now I can hate the man as well as his classification system.

Curator of the Chinese collections in the British Library, FRANCES WOOD is aware that she is not entitled to call herself a librarian as she has never taken any library exams. She thus avoided the humiliation suffered by her father who managed to fail his (because they were so boring) but nonetheless ended his career as Principal Keeper of the Department of Printed Books in the British Library.

Coming attractions . . .

P. D. JAMES remembers a tragedy at law

PETER OSBORNE takes a short walk down Fleet Street

ANNE BOSTON visits the Finzi-Continis

SEBASTIAN PEAKE grows up with a genius

ROWAN PELLING falls for Nigel Balchin

ARIANE BANKES goes to the wars

HUMPHREY AND SOLVEIG STONE recall M.K.L. Fisher

Bibliography